Every one who
knows the Law and
becomes a
disciple of the
kingdom of Heaven
is like a householder
who can produce
from his store both
the new and the old.
Matthew 13:52
(Phillips)

The Radical Wesley

& Patterns for Church Renewal

Howard A. Snyder

INTER-VARSITY PRESS
DOWNERS GROVE
ILLINOIS 60515

InterVarsity Press is the book-publishing division of Inter-Varsity Christian Fellowship, a student movement active on campus at hundreds of universities, colleges and schools of nursing. For information about local and regional activities, write IVCF, 233 Langdon St., Madison, WI 53703

Distributed in Canada through InterVarsity Press, 1875 Leslie St., Unit 10, Don Mills, Ontario M3B 2M5, Canada.

ISBN 0-87784-625-1

Printed in the United States of America

Library of Congress Cataloging in Publication Data
Snyder, Howard A
    The radical Wesley and patterns for church renewal.

    Based in part on the author's thesis, Notre Dame.
    Includes bibliographical references and index.
    1. Wesley, John, 1703-1791. 2. Methodist
Church–Clergy–Biography. 3. Clergy–England–
Biography. 4. Church. 5. Church renewal.
I. Title.
BX8495.W5S56   287'.092'4 [B]   80-18197
ISBN 0-87784-625-1

---

17 16 15 14 13 12 11 10 9 8 7 6 5 4 3 2 1
94 93 92 91 90 89 88 87 86 85 84 83 82 81 80

For Janice

CONTENTS

Preface

Perhaps Western culture is nearing a point where the Christian faith can be successfully reintroduced. Maybe the collapse of the present order will lead to a new outbreak of revolutionary Christianity. The publisher of Rolling Stone *wrote recently, "Since politics, economics and war have failed to make us feel any better—as individuals or as a nation—and we look back at long years of disrepair, then maybe the time for religion has come again."*[1]

Two centuries ago in England John Wesley saw God's providence at work in the way Deism had undermined traditional Christianity in his day. "This was the most direct way," he wrote, "whereby nominal *Christians could be prepared, first, for tolerating, and, afterwards, for receiving,* real *Christianity"—by "causing a total disregard for all religion, to pave the way for the revival of the only religion which was worthy of God!"*[2]

This, in part, is what the present book is about. Readers of my previous books, The Problem of Wineskins *and* The Community of the King, *will recognize that this little volume deals with similar questions, but in a different way. In* Wineskins *I briefly explored the Wesleyan witness in eighteenth-century England as one example of church renewal. This book continues that exploration in greater depth.*

Who am I writing for? I write for those sidetracked "mainline"

Christians by whom, as Albert Outler says, John Wesley "has been revered but not carefully studied." I write for some immobilized heirs of the Holiness Movement who still see Wesley through the lens of his nineteenth-century interpreters and for non-Wesleyan evangelicals who like Wesley's results but not his theology. I write for charismatic sisters and brothers who (often unknowingly) stand in one branch of the Wesleyan tradition and to whom Wesley would speak both encouragement and caution. I write for radical biblical Christians who can find in Wesley both a hero and a helper toward a more inclusive view of the church, and for church growth enthusiasts who in their pragmatism sometimes neglect to ask what the church really is. And I expect I also write for what seems to be a new movement of "orthodox evangelicals," those calling for a reaffirmation of historic Christianity, but with a strongly evangelical thrust.[3] The book may have special interest for such folks, since this is the very thing Wesley specialized in.

Finally, I write to help answer my own questions as I continue my quest to understand God's plan through the church (Eph. 3:9-10).

I am grateful to those who have provided the impulse and motivation to pursue this study. A special word of thanks goes to Joe Culumber, a brother with whom I have studied Wesley's sermons over the past two years and whose dialog with me on Wesley has been most helpful. Thanks also go to Light and Life Men International for permitting me, while serving as executive director, to pursue the doctoral study at the University of Notre Dame out of which, in part, this book takes its rise.

The Foundry, Moorfields, London
The First Methodist Class Meeting, Bristol, 1742

Susannah Wesley and the Epworth Parishioners   John Wesley Preaching from a Market Cross

Charles Wesley

John Wesley Preaching on His Father's Tomb at Epworth

The First Methodist Conference, 1744

Specimens of Early Methodist Class Tickets

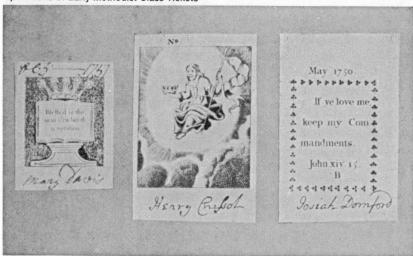

INTRODUCTION:
NEW-BUT-OLD TRUTHS

It is early Sunday morning, May 30, 1742. The northern port city of Newcastle-upon-Tyne is hardly awake. Two strangers from London, one a slight man in his late thirties, walk quietly down Sandgate Street in "the poorest and most contemptible part of the town."[1]

The two men stop at the end of the street and begin singing the Hundredth Psalm. A few curious people gather, and the shorter man starts preaching from Isaiah 53:5—"He was wounded for our transgressions, he was bruised for our iniquities: the chastisement of our peace was upon him; and with his stripes we are healed."

The knot of listeners grows to a crowd of several hundred, then over a thousand. When the small man stops, the crowd gapes in astonishment. So the preacher announces: "If you desire to know who I am, my name is John Wesley. At five in the evening, with God's help, I design to preach here again."[2]

That night Wesley finds a crowd of some 20,000 waiting. After he preaches many urge him to stay longer, at least for a few days. But Wesley has to leave at three o'clock the next morning to keep an appointment elsewhere.[3]

So begins Wesley's work in Newcastle, henceforth to be the northern point in his annual triangular tour of England. For nearly fifty years he will make a yearly circuit from London to Bristol to Newcastle and back to London, preaching and teaching daily, with many side trips along the way.

Organized to Beat the Devil It is hard to grasp all that is happening in this one small incident. Perhaps a present-day comparison will help. Suppose Billy Graham were to show up, alone and unannounced, with no advertising or sophisticated preparations, in Chicago's worst ghetto and begin preaching from the sidewalk. Wesley's first appearance in Newcastle was something like that. And this basic pattern Wesley followed for several decades, all over England.

Wesley, the master organizer, never built a great evangelistic organization. He simply went everywhere preaching, and he sent out other preachers in similar pattern. Wesley's gift for organization was bent toward the one objective of forming a genuine people of God within the institutional church. He concentrated not on the efforts *leading up to* decision but on the time *after* decision. His system had little to do with publicity or public image but everything to do with building the community of God's people. From the beginning of Wesley's great ministry in 1738, the secret of his radicality lay in his forming little bands of God-seekers who joined together in an earnest quest to be Jesus' disciples. He "organized to beat the devil"[4]—not to make converts but to turn converts into saints. Wesley would have nothing of "solitary religion," secret Christians or faith without works.

Many years later Wesley wrote, "In religion I am for as few innovations as possible. I love the old wine best."[5] Yet Wesley was one of the great innovators of church history. Although eighty-six when he made this remark, he could have said the same thing fifty years earlier.

The remark is, in fact, typical of Wesley's whole ecclesiology, his view of the church. The key words are "as possible." Hold to the old. But if the old hinders the gospel, then changes and innovations must be made. Wesley's ecclesiology was a working synthesis of old and new, tradition and innovation.

Perhaps the church today can learn new things from John Wesley. People, even the born-again kind, are notoriously weak at holding together paradoxes which belong together—like the Spirit and the Word, the private and the social, or "things old and new" (Mt. 13:52). Yet true renewal in the church always weds new insights, ideas and methods with the best elements from history. And true renewal is always a return, at the most basic level, to the ideal of the church as presented in Scripture and as lived out in a varying mosaic of faithfulness and unfaithfulness down through history. John Wesley represents an intriguing synthesis of old and new, conservative and radical, tradition and innovation that can spark greater clarity in today's new quest to be radically Christian.

By any standards, John Wesley was a remarkable man. His life (1703-91) nearly spanned the eighteenth century. From the time he began "field preaching" in 1739 until his death fifty-two years later he traveled some 225,000 miles and preached more than 40,000 times, sometimes to crowds of more than 20,000.[6] At his death he left behind 72,000 Methodists in Great Britain and Ireland and a fledgling Methodist denomination in America of some 57,000 members.[7] According to C. E. Vulliamy, Wesley was the "ascendant personality" of his age, more widely known in Britain than any other Englishman of the time.[8]

But the reasons for studying Wesley today go beyond mere historical curiosity. Wesley's role in bringing spiritual renewal to a rapidly industrializing society and his understanding and practice of Christian discipleship suggest two aspects of his continuing relevance.[9] If anything, Wesley is more significant today than for any period since the eighteenth century. He is important—and often cited—as an example of warm-hearted evangelism tied to active social reform. His historical and theological significance is being reassessed—witness Bernard Semmel's 1973 book, *The Methodist Revolution,* the theme of the Sixth Oxford Institute of Methodist Theological Studies in 1977, "Sanctification and Liberation," and a spate of new books. And now, after two hundred years, an Oxford edition of Wesley's works is finally being published.

A Rising Star Signs of growing appreciation of John Wesley *precisely as a theologian* are evident today. Wesleyans have sometimes been rather apologetic about Wesley's theological work, saying that, after all, Wesley did not attempt to write a systematic theology.[10] True. But perhaps this is Wesley's strength, not his weakness. Theologians tend to admire other theologians who have neat and profound systems. Calvin's theological reputation rests especially on his accomplishment as a logical systematizer. Therefore other theologians like to study him, and a large literature on Calvinism exists. By contrast, Wesley has been considered a second-rate theologian. It has sufficed to say, "As a theologian, Wesley was a great revivalist!" The literature on Wesley is primarily historical and biographical, rather than theological. Over 200 biographies or biographical studies on Wesley have come from the presses.[11]

Two new-but-old truths are dawning on us today, however. First, theology must be grounded in life. It must be tied to and spring from *praxis,* as the Latin American theologians have been insisting. Secondly, theology is not just the work of "theologians." It is the task of the whole body of Christ. All Christians are called to be theologians, if by this we mean all believers should be literate about the biblical faith and know how to apply that faith intelligently to all of life. Further, theology must grow out of the witness and community life of the church. Perhaps we are on the verge of a fuller recovery of the priesthood of believers precisely at the point of theology.

For these and other reasons, Wesley's theological star is rising. As A. Skevington Wood observes, "For too long it has been assumed that the founder of Methodism was mainly a man of action and only minimally a man of constructive thought. Recent years, however, have witnessed a radical reappraisal of his theological role, which in turn has required that the nature of his distinctive doctrinal emphasis should be taken into serious consideration."[12]

This book looks at Wesley both as practitioner and as theologian. For in Wesley theology and practice *really were* one. From the beginning, his theological work grappled with practical issues. His theology was shaped by his experience, and he most earnestly cared that his action be grounded in sound doctrine.

The Shape of Life Together   For several years I have felt that *ecclesiology*—the doctrine of the church—is basic for biblical faith. The growing stress today on discipleship, lifestyle, church growth and similar concerns further confirms this conviction. We are coming to see that a soteriology (doctrine of salvation) stripped of a biblical ecclesiology cannot be fully biblical. The key question is: What is the shape of our life together as the people of God in the world?

I believe Wesley can help us precisely at these points. So this book examines John Wesley—not just Wesley the Anglican but also Wesley the radical. My aim is to understand Wesley better by viewing him from an angle too often ignored and to search for insights needed in the contemporary church.

Many Christians seeking a new speaking-forth and living-out of the gospel today have rediscovered the Anabaptist or Radical Protestant tradition. Anabaptism, as Wes Michaelson of *Sojourners* writes,

has provided a unique point of identification for many from an evangelical heritage who are taking the call to discipleship seriously in our time. This is because of the pivotal questions which, historically, Anabaptism has asked and attempted to answer:

What does it mean to give our lives according to all the demands of the gospel?

How can our lives be molded consistently by the pattern of Christ's servanthood?

What are the concrete implications of loving our enemies?

How is the church to live out its life as a called community of God's people?

The evangelical tradition has generally evaded these questions; only in the last few years have such concerns even entered evangelical discourse. Anabaptism has urgently asked those questions for centuries.[13]

Though rooted in a rather different context from historic Anabaptism, John Wesley asked similar questions. In comparing Wesley with the Radical Reformers of Luther's and Zwingli's day, in fact, I note a number of arresting parallels—as well as some important differences. John Wesley represents in his own right a form of radical Christianity, a rather unique blend of diverse elements that deserves closer scrutiny.

The relation between early Methodism and Anabaptism remains largely unexplored. Since two hundred years and major cultural differences separate the two movements and there are almost no direct historical links, it is easy to assume that little or no relationship exists between the sixteenth-century "radicals" and the eighteenth-century English evangelical revivalists. This book suggests that a significant relationship does in fact exist, and that it hinges primarily on ecclesiological questions rather than on historical continuity. The purpose of the book is, in part, to explore this relationship.

With the Radical Reformers, and especially the Anabaptists, the question of the meaning of the church was central, so much so that Franklin Littell entitled his ground-breaking study of Anabaptism *The Anabaptist View of the Church.*[14] The

Radical Reformers wanted to carry the Reformation clear through to a radical restructuring of the life and experience of the Christian community. So did John Wesley. In this sense Wesley stands in the Radical Protestant tradition. Yet he lived and died an Anglican and hoped for a general reformation of the church. He was a radical reformer of a different stripe.

Wesley's practice grew out of his view of the church. So we need to know what that view was. Although Wesley "did not attempt to formulate a new doctrine of the church but to remedy its decadence," as Frank Baker notes,[15] still his ministry of renewal forced him to face ecclesiological questions continually. His concept of the church has been variously labeled Catholic, Anglican, Classical Protestant, Puritan and free church; and, as F. Ernest Stoeffler comments, "passages can be found in John Wesley's many writings which will support one or all of these interpretations."[16] Yet his ministry led to the birth of one of the largest free churches, and Wesley is, therefore, frequently seen as standing in the free church or Radical Protestant tradition.[17]

Part of Wesley's problem—or rather, our problem with Wesley—is that he doesn't fit the molds in which we place him. We are not used to a popular mass evangelist who is also a university scholar, speaks several languages, knows classical and Christian authors by heart, and publishes his own English dictionary. Nor are we any better prepared to handle an evangelist who is also a social reformer or a theologian who preaches several times daily, develops his own discipling and nurturing system, sends out teams of traveling preachers, and publishes a home medical handbook that goes through twenty-some editions!

In these pages I delve into Wesley's view of the church and Christian discipleship to see not only what Wesley believed, but also how his views may help earnest Christians today. It will be useful to note what Wesley has in common with historic Radical Protestantism, that stream of Christianity flowing from sixteenth-century Anabaptism but represented also by a broad range of free church or believers' church groups. I will not attempt to show direct historical links between Wesley and the Anabaptists nor to co-opt Wesley for an Anabaptistic understanding of radical Christianity. We want to examine Wesley on his own terms, for this is where his importance lies.

In this connection it is important to note that I use "Radical Protestant" and "believers' church" as fundamentally synonymous categories and ways of viewing the church. In this I follow Donald F. Durnbaugh in his significant 1968 study, *The Believers' Church: The History and Character of Radical Protestantism.*[18] Radical Protestantism consists of those church bodies which wanted to carry the Reformation through to a thorough restructuring of the church on a New Testament model. As representative Radical Protestant or believers' church groups, Durnbaugh discusses the Waldenses, the Unity of Brethren *(Unitas Fratrum)* and later Moravian Brethren, Anabaptist groups, and early Baptists, Quakers and Methodists. He also includes more recent groups such as the Disciples of Christ, Plymouth Brethren and the Confessing Church in Nazi Germany.

Three things need to be said about this perspective in order to clarify the later discussion. First, this is a thematic and typological approach, not one based on linear history. While significant historical links can be traced between many Radical Protestant groups, this is a secondary consideration. The important fact is the similar understanding of the church which distinguishes these groups, in spite of the differing historical settings.

Second, a word needs to be said about infant baptism. Since "Anabaptist" means "rebaptizer" and most believers' churches baptize adults and not infants, many interpreters place great weight on the practice of believers' baptism historically and miss the more fundamental issue: *voluntarism.* Franklin Littell notes that even in early Anabaptism the "real issue" was "not the act of baptism, but rather a bitter and irreducible struggle between two mutually exclusive concepts of the church." Anabaptists were "out to restore apostolic Christianity. Baptism became important because it was the most obvious dividing line between the two systems."[19] Similarly Leonard Verduin notes that the Anabaptist rejection of infant baptism was based primarily "on an aversion to 'christening,' that is, to baptism with sacralist overtones," and thus "early Anabaptism was not so much a matter of anti-pedobaptism as a matter of anti-Constantinianism." In fact, some of the early Anabaptists did not repudiate infant baptism at first, but only the christening ritual.[20]

It is well to bear this in mind when we examine early Methodism, where infant baptism was of course practiced. And it is well to remember in this connection that today virtually all Christian groups, Catholic and Protestant alike, are voluntary associations.

The third consideration concerns the place of the Moravian Brethren as representative of Radical Protestantism. The Moravians are seen here as carriers of the Radical Protestant strain in their contacts with John Wesley. This could be disputed if our main concern were with direct historical connections. The above discussion makes clear, however, that this is not our focus. With Durnbaugh, George H. Williams and others, I see the Moravians (and the earlier *Unitas Fratrum)* as standing within the Radical Protestant tradition because of their fundamental conception of the church.[21]

The general plan of the book is successively historical, theological and analytical. The first section tells the story of Wesley's formative years from 1725 to about 1745. The second examines Wesley's understanding of the church and its role in history. The final section discusses the life and renewal of the church today in the light of Wesley's concepts.

one

THE MAKING OF
A RADICAL CHRISTIAN

1

WESLEY'S
ROOTS

John Wesley's spiritual rebirth and the rise of Methodism occurred during the years 1738 to 1740. These years also mark the period of Wesley's most intimate contact with the Moravian Brethren.

Four crises hit Wesley during this time: (1) his sense of failure on returning from America in February 1738; (2) his "heart-warming experience" on May 24, 1738; (3) his confrontation with field preaching in April 1739; and (4) his break with the Fetter Lane Society on July 20, 1740. These crises set the direction of Wesley's life ministry, and they partly shaped his understanding of the church. These are the focus of this and the succeeding three chapters of this book. But first, in order to grasp these critical events, we must review Wesley's pilgrimage during the previous several years.

John Wesley's spiritual quest began in earnest in 1725. It started when, at his father's urging, Wesley began to study for ordination.[1] The direction of his quest was clear from the beginning: "I began to aim at, and pray for, inward holiness."[2] Seeking holiness in every area of life, he began his lifelong custom of weekly communion.[3]

Wesley was ordained a deacon in the Church of England in September 1725 and priest in July 1728. In the intervening years he was elected a fellow of Lincoln College, Oxford (1726), and received his Master of Arts degree (1727). He read extensively during this period and was strongly attracted toward mysticism. He encountered William Law's *Serious Call to a Devout and Holy Life* shortly after it was published in 1728. Vulliamy notes that "the *Serious Call* played its part in confirming the habits of personal discipline and of pious exclusion which marked the life of Wesley at Oxford from 1729 to 1735" and strengthened his mystical leanings "until the Moravian example gave to Wesley's religious life an essentially practical tendency."[4]

Wesley was at Oxford almost constantly from 1729 until 1735, teaching, tutoring and studying. He quickly became the leader of the "Holy Club," which his brother Charles had organized there with two others. This religious cell flourished until the Wesley brothers left for Georgia in 1735. One of the members was George Whitefield.

The Holy Club was simply "a society of very young and very earnest High Churchmen, with evangelistic views and a true desire to lead the lives of exemplary Christians."[5] Its primary aim was the spiritual development of its members. Wesley wrote to his father in 1734, "My one aim in life is to secure personal holiness, for without being holy myself I cannot promote real holiness in others."[6] Good works were an expression of this desire for holiness. The Wesleys and their colleagues visited prisoners and poor families, helped them financially and began school classes for poor children.[7]

The Religious Societies In founding the Holy Club the Wesleys followed the religious society pattern which had grown up in the Church of England over the previous forty years. Anthony Horneck, an influential Anglican preacher who had come to England from the Continent around 1661, first organized such cells for earnest young Anglicans about 1678.[8] This was about the time Philip Jacob Spener, whom

Horneck had known in Germany, published his *Pia Desideria* (1675) and began forming small devotional cells in Germany called *collegia pietatis,* giving rise to German Pietism.[9]

In England the Anglican religious societies spread and became a mini-renewal movement. At least forty such societies were meeting in the London area by the early 1700s.[10] Besides observing strict devotional rules, religious society members "visited the poor at their houses and relieved them, fixed some in a way of trade, set prisoners at liberty, furthered poor scholars at the University,"[11] and established scores of charity schools for the poor. Richard Heitzenrater notes that by 1700 "this form of religious organization had established itself with[in] the structure of the Church as a viable expression of Christian piety and social concern." Despite its institutional deadness, "the Church of England made a concerted effort to secure such reforming zeal within its own structure" by permitting and encouraging these societies.[12] The special concern of the religious societies for the poor and disadvantaged is especially noteworthy in light of later Methodism.

The Wesley brothers were well acquainted with this movement. Their father had long been an ardent supporter of religious societies. Samuel Wesley, pastor at Epworth, had in fact organized a society for promoting Christian knowledge in his parish in 1702, following the pattern of the newly founded Society for Promoting Christian Knowledge (SPCK).[13] The purpose of the Epworth society, wrote Samuel Wesley, was "First to pray to God; Secondly, to read the Holy Scriptures, and discourse upon Religious Matters for their mutual Edification; and Thirdly, to deliberate about the Edification of our neighbour, and the promoting of it."[14] The outward ministry to "our neighbour" was by no means neglected. The society's rules included the following:

Their first care is to set Schools for the Poor, wherein Children (or if need be, Adult Persons) may be instructed in the Fundamentals of Christianity by men of known and approv'd Piety.

Their second design is to procure little Practical Treatises from Holland, England, and Germany, &c. to translate them into the Vulgar Tongue, print them, and so to give or lend them to those who are less solicitous of their own and others Edification.

The Third is to establish a Correspondence with such Societies in England, Germany, &c. that so they may mutually Edify one another. . . .

The Fourth is to take Care of the Sick and other Poor, and to afford them Spiritual as well as Corporal Helps.[15]

Samuel Wesley was quick to see not only the practical value of such societies but also something of their significance in church history. In a "Letter Concerning the Religious Societies" he wrote,

I know few good Men but lament that after the Destruction of Monasteries, there were not some Societies founded in their stead, but reformed from their Errors, and reduced to the Primitive Standard. None who has but lookt into our own Church-History, can be ignorant how highly instrumental such Bodies of Men as these, were to the first planting and propagating Christianity amongst our Forefathers. . . . A great part of the good Effects of that way of Life, may be attained without many of the Inconveniences of it, by such Societies as we are now discoursing of.[16]

The benefits of monasticism without its "inconveniences"! This was the goal of the elder Wesley—and later of his most prominent son.

What Samuel Wesley only dreamed and talked of doing, however, his remarkable wife Susannah carried out, at least in a measure. Samuel Wesley often traveled to London on church and political business, leaving Susannah and the large family alone at Epworth. In early 1712, while Samuel was on a prolonged absence, Susannah began a small meeting in the parsonage. As she related in letters to her husband, the meeting grew out of the family devotional time Susannah held on Sunday evenings with her children. A few neighbors asked to attend, then others, so that the group soon grew from about thirty persons to over 200. At these gatherings Mrs. Wesley would read a sermon, pray and talk with the people who came.[17]

This new venture caused a stir in Epworth and some friction between Susannah and her husband. Samuel liked the theory but not the practice. He objected to these home meetings because they were led by a woman, might cause him some embarrassment and would be seen by some as a "conventicle," a private, separatist religious gathering.

Susannah defended herself in two masterful letters to her husband on February 6 and 25, 1712. She noted that attendance at the church services had jumped dramatically due to her meetings despite the opposition (and jealousy?) of Mr. Inman, Wesley's assistant. Mrs. Wesley wrote,

This one thing has brought more people to church than ever any thing did in so short a time. We used not to have above twenty or twenty-five at evening service, whereas now we have between two and three hundred; which are more than ever came to hear Inman in the morning.

Besides the constant attendance on the public worship of God, our meeting has wonderfully conciliated the minds of this people towards us, so that we now live in the greatest amity imaginable; and what is still better, they are very much reformed in their behavior on the Lord's day; and those who used to be playing in the streets, now come to hear a good sermon read, which is surely more acceptable to Almighty God.

Another reason for what I do, is, that I have no other way of conversing with this people, and therefore have no other way of doing them good; but by this I have an opportunity of exercising the greatest and noblest charity, that is, charity to their souls.

And she warned,

I need not tell you the consequences, if you determine to put an end to our meeting. . . . I can now keep [the people] to the church, but if it be laid aside, I doubt they will never go to hear him [Inman] more, at least those who came from the lower end of the town. . . .

If you do, after all, think fit to dissolve this assembly, do not tell me that you desire me to do it, for that will not satisfy my conscience: but send me your positive command, in such full and express terms, as may absolve me from all guilt and punishment for neglecting this opportunity of doing good, when you and I shall appear before the great and awful tribunal of our LORD JESUS CHRIST.[18]

The meetings seem to have continued until Samuel Wesley returned from London, but apparently not afterwards. Samuel lacked the insight, skill and openness which would have allowed him to perceive what was really happening and the similarities between what Susannah was doing and his intention for religious societies. So he was kept from benefiting from these home meetings and making them part of his pastoral work. Still, one already sees hints here of the dynamic which would be released two decades later under the leadership of Susannah's sons, John and Charles Wesley.

The Holy Club During John Wesley's teaching days at Oxford University the Holy Club observed a strict discipline which John himself devised, but which followed closely the pattern of other similar societies.

The members of the Club spent an hour, morning and evening, in private prayer. At nine, twelve and three o'clock they recited a collect, and at all times they examined themselves closely, watching for signs of grace, and trying to preserve a high degree of religious fervour. They made use of pious ejaculations, they frequently consulted their Bibles, and they noted, in cipher [that is, coded] diaries, all the particulars of their daily employment. One hour each day was set apart for meditation. . . . They fasted twice a week, observed all the feasts of the Church, and received the Sacraments every Sunday. Before going into company they prepared their conversation, so that words might not be spoken without purpose. The Primitive Church, in so far as they had knowledge of it, was to be taken as their pattern.[19]

Small wonder that Wesley and his companions were mockingly called "Methodists," "Sacramentarians," "Enthusiasts,"

"Bible Moths," the "Reforming Club" and "Supererogation Men." The name "Holy Club" was apparently the most popular tag among Oxford students, but the term "Methodist" was the one that stuck permanently to the Wesleys.[20]

So began "the people called Methodists," though the Methodist Revival was still a decade away. In labeling the Wesleys and their friends "Methodists" their mockers drew on a common fund of derisive names. A century earlier traditionalists had derided the "Anabaptists and plain packstaff Methodists" and others who stood for plainness and carefulness in life.[21]

John Wesley led a Spartan existence at Oxford. He lived on twenty-eight pounds a year, giving away all he did not need for clothing and sustenance. In one year he gave away sixty-two pounds; in another, ninety-two.[22] During these days Wesley developed many traits and disciplines which he kept throughout his life.

Off to Georgia   On a trip to London in 1735 the Wesley brothers met Colonel James Oglethorpe, an adventurer and philanthropist who was organizing a group to help settle his new colony in Georgia. The Wesleys agreed to go along, John as a missionary to the Indians and Charles as Oglethorpe's secretary. In October they set sail for the New World. Without their leadership the Holy Club at Oxford began to disintegrate.

The Gentleman's Magazine for October 1735 reported:
Tuesday 14, This morning James Oglethorpe Esq. accompanied by the Rev. Mr. John Wesley Fellow of Lincoln College, the Rev. Mr. Charles Wesley, Student of Christ Church College, and the Rev. Mr. Ingham of Queens College, Oxford, set out from Westminster to Gravesend, in order to embark for the Colony of Georgia–Two of the aforesaid Clergymen design, after a short stay in Savannah, to go amongst the Indian Nations bordering upon that Settlement, in order to bring them to the Knowledge of Christianity.[23]

John Wesley went to Georgia primarily, he said, to save his

own soul and learn the true meaning of the gospel by preaching to the Indians. He was sponsored by the Anglican Society for the Propagation of the Gospel at a salary of fifty pounds per year.[24] Characteristically, he didn't go alone. He joined with Charles and two friends, Benjamin Ingham and Charles Delamotte, to form what amounted to a Methodist Holy Club aboard the ship. Three of the four (all except Delamotte) had been Oxford Methodists, so in effect the Holy Club continued in this small shipboard band. John at thirty-two was the oldest of the four; Ingham and Delamotte were in their early twenties. On leaving England the four companions made the following covenant:

We, whose names are underwritten, being fully convinced that it is impossible, either to promote the work of God among the heathen, without an entire union among ourselves, or that such a union should subsist, unless each one will give up his single judgment to that of the majority, do agree, by the help of God: –first, that none of us will undertake anything of importance without first proposing it to the other three; –secondly, that whenever our judgments differ, any one shall give up his single judgment or inclination to the others; –thirdly, that in case of an equality [or tie], after begging God's direction, the matter shall be decided by lot.[25]

The little band followed a strict discipline including private prayer from four till five each morning, joint Bible study from five to seven and public prayers from eight till nine. From nine till noon Wesley usually studied German (so he could converse with the Moravians on board) while the other three were variously employed in study or teaching. The four met at noon for prayer and discussion and again at eight. The afternoons were spent in teaching the children and adults who would listen, while the hour from five to six was devoted to private prayer. The four went to bed between nine and ten in their two adjoining cabins.[26]

The long weeks on board ship to Georgia gave Wesley his first opportunity to observe the Moravian Brethren closely.

A small band of Moravian missionaries under the leadership of David Nitschmann was among the passengers. Normally Wesley spent the evening hour from seven to eight with them. Wesley noted in his Journal for Sunday, January 25, 1736, *At seven I went to the Germans [Moravians]. I had long before observed the great seriousness of their behaviour. Of their humility they had given a continual proof, by performing those servile offices for the other passengers which none of the English would undertake; . . . If they were pushed, struck, or thrown down, they rose again and went away; but no complaint was found in their mouth.*[27]

What impressed Wesley was not only the Moravians' piety and good works, but their calm assurance of faith during storms at sea—something he lacked. During his two years in Georgia he stayed in close contact with the Moravians, including the missionary August Spangenberg.

In Georgia, Wesley's zeal for holiness became "a burning desire to revitalize the church" and build "a model Christian community in one Anglican parish," as Frank Baker puts it.[28] Understandably, the rigor of his efforts in the lax frontier setting was not universally appreciated. Already, however, Wesley was introducing such innovations as hymn singing in public worship and the use of lay men and women in parish work.[29] Because of his zeal and his innovations he was accused of "leaving the Church of England by two doors at the same time"—Roman Catholicism and Puritan Separatism. But at heart his experiments simply sprang from his desire to recover the spirit and form of early Christianity.[30]

Wesley thought he saw in the Moravians some genuine elements, at least, of early Christianity, and he tried some of their methods. As Baker notes,

Wesley organized societies for religious fellowship quite apart from ordered public worship. In these gatherings the members spent about an hour in "prayer, singing and mutual exhortation," naturally under the close supervision whenever possible of their spiritual director. . . . Wesley even divided these societies into the "more intimate union" of "bands" after the Moravian pattern. It was this which readily fostered the charge of his having instituted a Roman Catholic confessional, for mutual confession was indeed one of the purposes of these small homogeneous groups.[31]

Here we see Wesley introducing a Moravian element into the religious society pattern he brought with him from England and being charged with Romanism!

Wesley's behavior in Georgia, as well as on board the *Simmonds,* should be seen also in light of his sponsorship by the Society for the Propagation of the Gospel. The SPG prescribed detailed rules for its missionaries, and Wesley followed these to the letter. On board ship missionaries were to "demean themselves . . . so as to become remarkable examples of piety and virtue to the ship's company." If possible they were to conduct daily morning and evening prayers with preaching and catechizing on Sundays, and they should "instruct, exhort, admonish and reprove as they have occasion and opportunity, with such seriousness and prudence, as may gain them reputation and authority."[32] At their place of service the SPG missionaries were (among other things) to study the doctrines and homilies of the Church of England and to carefully examine all candidates for baptism and the Lord's Supper. Richard Butterworth notes that much Wesley did in Georgia, including book distribution, starting schools, visiting outstations and seeking to reach the Indians, was "in exact obedience to the Instructions of the Society."[33]

Wesley spent two frustrating years in Georgia, however. His strictness and zeal made enemies of some, although it helped others. Then there was the complication of a frustrated romance. He went back to England in early 1738, arriving in London on February 3. He returned amid controversy, considering his missionary efforts a failure. He had been unable to evangelize any Indians.[34] He had stirred up opposition and controversy among the Anglican settlers. And he knew he lacked inward peace of soul.

2

ALDERSGATE AND FETTER LANE

The Moravian Brethren under Count Nicolaus von Zinzendorf were themselves an infant movement in 1738. But already they had contacts in England. The Moravian historian Holmes relates, "At a very early period after the Renewal of their Church, the Brethren formed pleasing acquaintances in England. To meet the wishes of some persons in London, who desired information of the establishment at Herrnhut, a deputation was sent thither in 1728."[1]

A few years later, in 1734, a group of Moravian missionaries arrived in London seeking permission from the Trustees of Georgia to go to America for the sake of religious liberty and "an opportunity of preaching the gospel."[2] A second group of twenty-six reached London in 1735. It was this group which sailed on the *Simmonds* with the Wesleys to Georgia. Zinzendorf himself visited London in 1737 and organized a Moravian "Diaspora Society," as he called it.[3]

The historian Holmes speaks of the "renewal" of the Moravian Church. In Wesley's day Moravianism was a new movement with ancient roots. The church's early history traces back to John Hus (c. 1372-1415), Peter Chelcicky (c. 1390-1460) and the Bohemian Brethren or *Unitas Fratrum*. It is here in fact that some scholars see the beginning of the believers' church idea.[4]

In 1722 a small remnant of the *Unitas Fratrum* from Moravia settled on the estate of Count Zinzendorf in Germany.[5] Zinzendorf (1700-60) was a Lutheran whose family had been closely associated with Philip Jacob Spener and other German Pietist leaders. He felt uniquely called to extend the message and experience of salvation by faith to the whole world. He organized the *Unitas Fratrum* remnant into the Renewed Church of the United Brethren, which became commonly known simply as the Moravian Brethren. Zinzendorf founded the Moravian settlement of Herrnhut ("the Lord's Watch") on his own estate, and this became the primary model for later Moravian communities. By 1733 he had started communities in two other locations as well and soon was sending small groups of Moravians overseas as missionary communities.[6]

Zinzendorf saw these new Moravian communities as a way to extend dramatically the *ecclesiolae in ecclesia* or "little churches within the church" approach to church renewal. The Moravian Brethren would be not a new or separate church but a dynamic missionary force throughout Christendom. Many young university types with no Moravian background, such as Peter Böhler and August Spangenberg, as others, responded to Zinzendorf's zeal and idealism and joined the Moravian movement. Soon Moravian missionaries, including those Wesley encountered in London and on board ship to the New World, were traveling far and wide.

Böhler and Aldersgate When Wesley returned to London in 1738 he met the young Moravian missionary Peter Böhler. Under date of February 7 Wesley recorded in his Journal, "I met Peter Böhler [and others], . . . just then landed from Germany. Finding they had no acquaintance in England, I offered to procure them a lodging, and did so near Mr. Hutton's, where I then was."[7]

Peter Böhler (1712-75), twenty-five when Wesley met him, was an effective *Bändhalter,* or Band-organizer, for the Moravians. Formerly a Lutheran, he had become acquainted with the Moravians while studying at the University of Jena. His spiritual awakening came after he heard Spangenberg, then a professor at Jena, lecture on a tract by Philip Spener, the Pietist leader. Böhler spent his life in Moravian missionary work in America and England.[8]

Wesley must have been impressed with Böhler on at least two counts: his convincing presentation of instantaneous conversion by faith alone and his practical organizing skill. In many ways, including his erudition, Böhler was much like Wesley. The two men walked and talked frequently from the time of their first encounter until Böhler sailed for America on May 4. Both John and Charles accompanied the young Moravian to Oxford on February 17, but they were puzzled by his views. Böhler wrote Zinzendorf, "I travelled with the two brothers, John and Charles Wesley, from London to Oxford. The elder, John, is a good-natured man; he knew he did not properly believe on the Saviour, and was willing to be taught."[9]

Böhler spent some days at Oxford and organized a band there. Wesley had further discussions with him both there and later at London. In March Wesley recorded, "I was, on *Sunday* the 5th, clearly convinced of unbelief, of the want of that faith whereby alone we are saved."[10]

About this time Wesley began a worship practice which was later much criticized as irregular: extemporaneous prayer. He noted on April 1, "Being at Mr. Fox's society [at Oxford], my heart was so full that I could not confine myself to the forms of prayer which we were accustomed to use there. Neither do I purpose to be confined to them any more; but to pray indifferently, with a form or without, as I may find suitable to particular occasions."[11]

These were critical days for Wesley. He was seeking the true understanding and experience of salvation by faith. He reread the New Testament in Greek and discovered that instantaneous conversions did indeed take place in the New Testament church. He talked with Böhler again on April 26, and Böhler later recorded, "He wept bitterly and asked me to pray with him. I can freely affirm, that he is a poor, broken-hearted sinner, hungering after a better righteousness than that which he had thus far had, even the righteousness of Christ."[12] Böhler reported that Wesley was one among several who were seeking a closer fellowship and therefore wanted to organize a "band," or small cell group.

On May 1 Wesley records, "This evening our little society began, which afterwards met in Fetter Lane."[13] This was the beginning of the Fetter Lane Society, of which more will be said shortly.

Wesley "broke the faith barrier" (as one has written[14]) on Wednesday, May 24, 1738, about three weeks after Böhler departed for America. His famous heart-warming experience came during a meeting in Aldersgate Street, and Wesley himself saw the experience as the critical turning point in his spiritual quest. "I felt I did trust in Christ, Christ alone for salvation; and an assurance was given me that He had taken away *my* sins, even *mine*, and saved *me* from the law of sin and death."[15] It is worth noting that this crucial experience, from which so much was to follow, occurred in the context of a small religious society meeting.

James Hutton (1715-95), bookseller, was a key figure both in the Aldersgate Street group and in the Fetter Lane Society, and an important link between Wesley and the Moravians. He had been moved by John Wesley's life and preaching before Wesley left for Georgia, and through Wesley he met the Moravian band embarking for Georgia in 1735. When in London the Wesleys often stayed with Hutton, and his home and bookshop, "The Bible and Sun," became a chief point of contact between the Wesleys and Moravians passing through London or living there.[16] Hutton had organized a religious society which met on Wednesday evenings in Aldersgate

Street and at which Moravian letters and diaries from Georgia were read. It seems likely that this was the meeting Wesley attended on May 24.[17]

As already noted, religious societies were common in England at this time, although as a movement they were in decline. The Fetter Lane Society, as well as the Holy Club and numerous other societies Wesley formed or was involved in, have to be seen in this context. But the Fetter Lane Society was also markedly Moravian in inspiration, due especially to the influence of Peter Böhler.

The Fetter Lane Society   Precisely who organized the Fetter Lane Society and drew up its rules—Wesley or Böhler—is unclear. They both had a hand in it. It is true that "Fetter Lane was not a Moravian Society, but a Religious Society in connexion with the Church of England."[18] But it was precisely Zinzendorf's dream to build a network of such societies throughout the main bodies of the Christian church, without separating from them, and this would have been Böhler's intent as well. Perhaps from its beginning some members of the group had conflicting ideas as to just what this society should become. Those most closely associated with the Moravians probably understood and shared Zinzendorf's vision, while others saw the group simply as another of the many Anglican religious societies.

John and Charles Wesley, Hutton, Böhler and a few others met at Hutton's home on the evening of May 1 and organized the society at Böhler's suggestion.[19] The rules of the society were later printed with the title "orders of a Religious Society, meeting in Fetter-lane; in obedience to the command of God by St. James, and by the advice of Peter Böhler, 1738." Some "orders" or rules were adopted on May 1 and others on May 29 and September 25.[20]

"The command of God by St. James" refers to James 5:16— "Confess your faults one to another, and pray one for another, that ye may be healed." The verse was frequently cited as the biblical basis for small group gatherings, especially the bands.

The Fetter Lane Society's rules included weekly meetings for prayer and confession, division into bands of five to ten persons each, the right and duty of each person to speak freely, procedures for admitting new members, and provision for a monthly love feast from 7:00 to 10:00 p.m.[21] An agreed financial contribution was to be collected monthly. Though Wesley could not have foreseen it, the Fetter Lane Society was to become the "seedplot of the British Moravian Church, an *ecclesiola* which became an *ecclesia*."[22] And James Hutton became "the first English Moravian."

Wesley now had a newfound assurance of faith, a supportive group to share his life with and an expanding preaching ministry. Now, finally, he saw that his long-standing dream of a real restoration of primitive Christianity within the Church of England was possible. He wanted to learn more, however, from the Moravians and other German Pietists, and so on June 7 he "determined, if God should permit, to retire for a short time into Germany," as he had decided to do even before he left Georgia.[23]

Stoeffler calls Wesley's trip to Germany an "intentional study-tour of Pietist centers." Wesley, he says,

was not interested in learning any more about the nature of Moravian piety. . . . he had come to regard the life of faith which he had witnessed among the Moravians, and which he had now found himself, in the same light as did the Moravians. . . . To them the corporate aspect of conscious religious renewal through "living faith" signified, as it were, a recapturing of the life of faith of the primitive Christian community. Their diaspora societies, therefore, were interpreted as nothing more and nothing less than a very much needed means of restoring the koinonia, the spirit, the message, and the sense of mission of that community within a given religious establishment, and of doing so without the need of disrupting the order of that establishment. What his study-trip to the Continent did for Wesley, then, was to afford him an opportunity to see the diaspora arrangement of the Moravians (as well as the collegio pietatis *of church-related Pietism in general) in actual operation. Thus he now became fully aware of the possibilities of this arrangement for his own work as he began to envision that work.*[24]

Wesley went to the Continent in June 1738, met Zinzendorf at Marienborn and reached Herrnhut on August 1. He spent some days at Herrnhut and other centers.[25] He visited Halle where he met Professor Francke, son of August Hermann Francke (1663-1727), the prominent Pietist leader and founder of the Pietist orphanage and schools at Halle.[26] Returning to London, he recorded on September 17, "I began again to declare in my own country the glad tidings of salvation."[27]

A letter to "the Church of God which is in Herrnhut" written some weeks later reveals both Wesley's appreciation for the Moravians and his own growing ministry:

We are endeavouring here also, by the grace which is given us, to be followers of you, as ye are of Christ. Fourteen were added to us, since our return, so that we have now eight bands of men, consisting of fifty-six persons [at Fetter Lane]; all of whom seek for salvation only in the blood of Christ. As yet we have only two small bands of women; the one of three and the other of five persons. But here are many others who only wait till we have leisure to instruct them, how they may most effectually build up one another in the faith and love of Him who gave himself for them.

Though my brother and I are not permitted to preach in most of the churches in London, yet (thanks be to God!) there are others left, wherein we have liberty to speak the truth as it is in Jesus. Likewise on every evening, and on set evenings in the week at two several places, we publish the word of reconciliation, sometimes to twenty or thirty, sometimes to fifty or sixty, sometimes to three or four hundred persons, met together to hear it.[28]

Having seen Herrnhut, Wesley had a great appreciation for Moravian faith and piety. He was uneasy, however, about their "quietism," their tendency toward spiritual complacency, and the "personality cult" which had grown up around Count Zinzendorf.[29] He now threw himself wholeheartedly into itinerant evangelism and care of converts in the London area, and seems to have assumed the primary leadership of the Fetter Lane Society with James Hutton as his chief lieutenant.

Two early 1739 *Journal* entries suggest something of the nature of the embryonic renewal:

Jan. 1, Mon. *Mr. Hall, Kinchin, Ingham, Whitefield, Hutchins, and my brother Charles were present at our lovefeast in Fetter Lane, with about sixty of our brethren. About three in the morning, as we were continuing instant in prayer, the power of God came mightily upon us, inasmuch that many cried out for exceeding joy, and many fell to the ground. As soon as we were recovered a little from that awe and amazement at the presence of His majesty we broke out with one voice, "We praise Thee, O God, we acknowledge Thee to be the Lord."*[30]

Two months later he wrote in London, "During my stay here I was fully employed between our own society in Fetter Lane and many others, where I was continually desired to expound."[31] Already Wesley was plugging into the existing network of religious societies. The flame was spreading from cell to cell. Submerged longings for a fresh taste of spiritual reality were starting to be met. The stir of a new awakening was in the air.

3

PREACHING TO
THE POOR

One hundred miles west of London was Bristol, a bustling port city of 30,000 people and the second city in the Kingdom in Wesley's day.[1] Located close to the Welsh border, it was the coal mining center which fed England's booming industrial revolution. Blossoming trade with the New World—including slaves—was bringing prosperity and debauchery to the growing city. Ale houses flourished; by 1736 over 300 were licensed, and this number grew to 384 by 1742.[2]

George Whitefield, evangelist and former Oxford colleague of the Wesleys, had just returned from preaching in America. Soon barred from London pulpits, he set off for Bristol. There on February 17, 1739, he preached for the first time in the open air to about 200 colliers (coal miners) at Kingswood. Within three weeks the crowds had mushroomed to 10,000, and Whitefield called on Wesley for help.[3]

Whitefield had been drawn to Bristol for three reasons. His home was nearby Gloucester on the Welsh border north of Bristol. He had been in touch with Howell Harris, leader of the Welsh revival which had begun some years earlier.[4] Then, too, turmoil and rioting had recently broken out among the coal miners of the region, particularly at Kingswood. When two of their leaders were arrested on January 19, soldiers were called out to secure the prisoners "in the face of all the mobbing women and amid a barrage of stones."[5]

The rioting around Bristol was part of a larger pattern of unrest during the period 1738-40 sparked by high corn prices, low wages and the oppressive poverty of the new class of urban workers. Although food riots erupted off and on throughout the century, historian Bernard Semmel notes that "the years 1739 and 1740, when Methodism erupted, were especially bad years" and the Kingswood miners were "regularly a source of difficulty."[6]

In these unsettled conditions Whitefield had immediate success in his preaching among the neglected Kingswood colliers. The ever watchful *Gentleman's Magazine* reported:

Bristol. *The Rev. Mr. Whitefield . . . has been wonderfully laborious and successful, especially among the poor Prisoners in Newgate, and the rude Colliers of Kingswood, preaching every day to large audiences, visiting, and expounding to religious Societies. On Saturday the 18th Instant he preach'd at Hannum Mount to 5 or 6000 Persons, amongst them many Colliers. In the Evening he removed to the Common, where . . . were crowded . . . a Multitude . . . computed at 20,000 People.*[7]

Whitefield's efforts did not go unnoticed or uncriticized. One alarmed London gentleman warned:

The Industry of the inferior People in a Society is the great Source of its Prosperity. But if one Man, like the Rev. Mr. Whitefield should have it in his Power, by his Preaching, to detain 5 or 6 thousands of the Vulgar from their daily Labour, what a Loss, in a little Time, may this bring to the Publick!—For my part, I shall expect to hear of a prodigious Rise in the Price of Coals, about the City of Bristol, if this Gentleman proceeds, as he has begun, with his charitable Lectures to the Colliers of Kingswood.[8]

Whitefield sent for John Wesley, recognizing his preaching power and organizing skill. Up to this point, however, Wesley had preached only in regular church services while in England. Should he accept Whitefield's appeal and help with the open-air meetings in Bristol? Charles thought not. But John submitted the decision to the Fetter Lane Society which cast lots and decided he should go.

Wesley's *Journal* for Saturday, March 31, reads:

In the evening I reached Bristol, and met Mr. Whitefield there. I could scarce reconcile myself at first to this strange way of preaching in the fields, of which he set me an example on Sunday; having been all my life (until very lately) so tenacious of every point relating to decency and order, that I should have thought the saving of souls almost a sin if it had not been done in a church.[9]

Sunday evening Wesley spoke to a little society on the Sermon on the Mount—"one pretty remarkable precedent of field-preaching," he observed, "though I suppose there were churches at that time also."[10] The next day, Monday, Wesley reports:

At four in the afternoon I submitted to be more vile, and proclaimed in the highways the glad tidings of salvation, speaking from a little eminence in a ground adjoining to the city, to about three thousand people. The scripture on which I spoke was this, . . . "The Spirit of the Lord is upon Me, because He hath anointed Me to preach the gospel to the poor."[11]

Characteristically, Wesley immediately began to organize. He formed a number of societies and bands and on May 9 acquired a piece of property where he built his "New Room" as a central meeting place.[12] When Whitefield returned to America in August, Wesley was left totally in charge of the growing work. He divided his time between Bristol and London, concentrating on open-air preaching, organizing bands and speaking at night to an increasing number of societies.

The Wesleyan Revival had begun. From the beginning it was a movement largely for and among the poor, those whom "gentlemen" and "ladies" looked on simply as part of the machinery of the new industrial system. The Wesleys preached, the crowds responded and Methodism as a mass movement was born.

Wesley soon discovered that some of his helpers had gifts for exhortation and preaching, and he put them to work. In 1744 he began a series of annual conferences with his preachers at which questions of doctrine, discipline and strategy were discussed. The minutes of the first conference show that Wesley quickly developed a general strategy for the movement. The "best way of spreading the Gospel," Wesley concluded, was "to go a little and a little farther from London, Bristol, St. Ives, Newcastle, or any other Society. So a little leaven would spread with more effect and less noise, and help would always be at hand."[13]

Wesley the Organizer Within a few months of beginning field preaching in 1739 Wesley had set up the basic structure that was to mark Methodism for over a century. The patterns he established formed the infrastructure of the movement and were crucial to its development and growth. They reveal something of Wesley's understanding of the church and sense of priorities. Wesley himself described how these forms originated in a 1748 letter which he called "A Plain Account of the People Called Methodists."[14]

The Society. Wesley's converts in London wished to meet with him regularly, and he was ready to comply. As numbers increased he quickly saw he could not visit them all individually in their homes, so he told them, "If you will all . . . come together every Thursday, in the evening, I will gladly spend some time with you in prayer, and give you the best advice I can." Wesley comments:

Thus arose, without any previous design on either side, what was afterwards called a Society; a very innocent name, and very common in London, for any number of people associating themselves together. . . . They therefore united themselves "in order to pray together, to receive the word of exhortation, and to watch over one another in love, that they might help each other to work out their salvation."

There is only one condition previously required in those who de-

sire admission into this society,—"a desire to flee from the wrath to come, to be saved from their sins."[15]

With this one simple entrance requirement, the Methodist society was at once the easiest and hardest group to join.

Wesley organized dozens of such societies in the London and Bristol areas. All the groups together were called the United Societies. As Wesley hints, he began building on the religious society pattern then common in England. He spoke often to existing religious societies in London and Bristol as well as organizing new Methodist societies. The French historian Elie Halévy notes,

It was, indeed, upon the Religious Societies in London and in the provinces that the two Wesleys and Whitefield first launched their propaganda. They found these societies numerous and flourishing; they succeeded so well in penetrating them with their influence that it is often difficult to say whether, . . . when the Methodists speak of a society, they mean a new association that they formed to spread their doctrine or one of the earlier Religious Societies that was now open, by the will of its members, to their new preaching.[16]

The main difference between the Methodist societies and the many other religious societies then functioning was that these were directly under the supervision of Wesley and were united chiefly in his person. Wesley was, of course, at this time still meeting with the Fetter Lane Society.

Of the rise of the Methodist societies Wesley says characteristically, "Upon reflection, I could not but observe, This is the very thing which was from the beginning of Christianity."[17]

The Band. Of all Wesley's innovations, the bands are most directly traceable to Moravian influence. Wesley had found numerous bands functioning at Herrnhut and as Baker notes, on his return he "enthusiastically advocated the system of 'bands' for all the religious societies in London, including that in Fetter Lane."[18] We have noted in Wesley's letter to Herrnhut that he reports ten bands meeting in the Fetter Lane

Society by October 1739 with an average membership of about six.

The bands were small cells of either men or women gathered for pastoral care. New converts were beset with temptations and needed both encouragement and opportunity for confession, Wesley noted.

These, therefore, wanted some means of closer union; they wanted to pour out their hearts without reserve, particularly with regard to the sin which did still easily beset them, and the temptations which were most apt to prevail over them. And they were the more desirous of this, when they observed it was the express advice of an inspired writer: "Confess your faults one to another, and pray for one another, that ye may be healed."

In compliance with their desire, I divided them into smaller companies; putting the married or single men, and married or single women, together.[19]

Rules for band societies were drawn up as early as December 1738.[20] Thus the bands actually preceded both the organized Methodist societies and the class meetings.

The Class Meeting. The Wesleyan class meeting arose in Bristol in early 1742 somewhat by accident. Wesley was increasingly concerned that many Methodists did not live the gospel; "several grew cold, and gave way to the sins which had long easily beset them." Clearly some mechanism for exercising discipline was needed.

To meet the preaching-house debt in Bristol, the society there (now numbering over 1,100) was divided into "classes" of a dozen each. Leaders were appointed to secure weekly contributions toward the debt, and Wesley, being Wesley, asked the leaders also to "make a particular inquiry into the behaviour of those whom he saw weekly."[21] This provided the opportunity for exercising discipline. Thus, says Wesley,

As soon as possible, the same method was used in London and all other places. Evil men were detected, and reproved. They were borne with for a season. If they forsook their sins, we received them gladly;

if they obstinately persisted therein, it was openly declared that they were not of us. The rest mourned and prayed for them, and yet rejoiced, that, as far as in us lay, the scandal was rolled away from the society.[22]

At first the class leaders visited the members in their homes, but this proved to be too time-consuming and somewhat complicated for several reasons, in part because of the poor and crowded conditions where many new converts lived. "Upon all these considerations it was agreed, that those of each class should meet all together. And by this means, a more full inquiry was made into the behaviour of each person."[23] And Wesley reflects:

It can scarce be conceived what advantages have been reaped from this little prudential regulation. Many now happily experienced that Christian fellowship of which they had not so much as an idea before. They began to "bear one another's burdens," and naturally to "care for each other." As they had daily a more intimate acquaintance with, so they had a more endeared affection for, each other. And "speaking the truth in love, they grew up into Him in all things, who is the Head, even Christ."[24]

This little statement bears reading and rereading. Note what is happening here. Through the small group structure of the class meeting, biblical descriptions of what *should* happen in the church sprang to life. Without this intimate form of community, believers were not, in fact, bearing one another's burdens; encouraging and exhorting one another; really coming to know each other; speaking the truth in love. The growth of the body was merely an abstract idea, as in so much contemporary Christianity (evangelical and otherwise). But once a structure and practice of community were instituted, the church began to function biblically as church, as body of Christ. Here is a lesson in the biblical reality of the church that has not been lost on those today who are calling for and experiencing true Christian community.

The class meetings were not designed merely as Christian

growth groups, however, or primarily as cells for koinonia, although in fact they did serve that function. Their primary purpose was discipline. The band had already been instituted as the primary spiritual cell of Methodism. As Skevington Wood observes, "The class was the disciplinary unit of the society" and was "the keystone to the entire Methodist edifice," while the band was the confessional unit. Wood adds, "This mutual confession to one another, based on the scriptural injunction of James 5:16, was the Methodist equivalent of auricular confession to a priest, and was designed to bring the same sense of relief and catharsis."[25]

In fact, such confession and mutual support in the context of close community produced a deeper level of healing than confession to an individual priest, by itself, could ever do.

All band and class members met together quarterly for the love feast, another Moravian contribution. A system of membership tickets was used, and only persons with tickets were admitted to the love feasts.[26]

Leaders in the Methodist movement now included the preachers and assistants Wesley appointed, class and band leaders, stewards, visitors of the sick, and schoolmasters. In providing for the care of the sick Wesley observed, "Upon reflection, I saw how exactly, in this also, we had copied after the primitive Church."[27]

In building the Methodist system Wesley was led to take measures he had not foreseen. Surveying the unshepherded crowds at Bristol, he determined "preaching the gospel to the poor" must take precedence over custom and "propriety." And as awakened sheep flocked to him for guidance, he adopted and adapted forms to keep the sheep folded and growing. And Wesley saw—in surprise and confirmation—that this was "the very thing" the New Testament church was all about.

4

A PEOPLE
CALLED METHODISTS

Wesley's heavy duties in the growing work at Bristol frequently kept him away from London. But whenever there he was active in the Fetter Lane Society and in looking after the expanding flock of Methodists.

The two Wesleys and James Hutton continued as the principal leaders at Fetter Lane until October 1739. In that month Philip Henry Molther arrived from the Continent. It was conflict between Wesley and Molther which led to Wesley's separation from the Fetter Lane Society in July 1740.

Break with the Moravians   As early as June 1739 Wesley was getting reports from London that the Fetter Lane Society was falling apart and needed him. Apparently some of the Moravian Brethren also saw the need for more consistent leadership and applied to Germany for help. This move and the mixed character of the society at this time are suggested by the Moravian historian Holmes:

At the request of the friends of the Brethren in London, one of their ministers, Philip Henry Molther, was appointed to care for the Society, which had been formed in the metropolis. The persons comprising this Society, were partly those, who had been excited to greater zeal in religion by the labors of the two Wesleys, and partly such as ascribed their spiritual attainments to their acquaintance with the Brethren.[1]

Molther had, in fact, arrived in London on October 18, 1739, on his way to Pennsylvania. A few days later James Hutton returned to London from a six-month visit to the Moravians in Germany, where he learned the German language and acquired a Moravian wife. Finding no ship bound immediately for the New World, Molther remained in London until late summer, 1740, and so became involved with the Fetter Lane Society.[2] A leadership and doctrinal struggle between John Wesley and Molther (and, secondarily, between Charles Wesley and Hutton) began at once.

Philip Molther (1714-80) was, like Böhler, a young Lutheran student at the University of Jena who had cast his lot with the Moravians and been ordained by them.[3] He taught a doctrine of "stillness" that ran directly counter to Wesley's emphasis on the means of grace. He began telling the Fetter Lane folks they did not truly have saving faith if they still felt any doubt or fear. They should therefore abstain from all the ordinances, particularly the Lord's Supper, and "be still" before the Lord until they received true faith. The ordinances are not really means of grace, he taught, for Christ is the only means. Charles Wesley commented, "He expressly denies that grace, or the Spirit, is transmitted through the means, particularly through the Sacrament."[4]

Molther, in other words, argued that most of the Fetter Lane members were defective in faith. Perhaps they had been awakened spiritually, but they were not truly converted. Therefore they should desist from everything else and wait in "stillness" until they received true faith. To Molther the sacraments were clearly less important than to Wesley with his Anglican understanding of the church. Wesley knew the Fetter Lane people well and felt many of them were born again and were growing spiritually. As always, his view of grace was dynamic. The new birth was a distinct event, but was preceded and followed by growth. The sacraments were God-given and helpful both to the seeker and to the Christian growing in sanctification. Wesley was therefore appalled at Molther's teaching and his discounting of what Wesley saw to be a genuine work of grace in the lives of many sincere people.[5]

August Spangenberg, the Moravian leader Wesley had known in Georgia, was then in London. Wesley went to see him on November 7. He was disturbed to find that Spangenberg seemed to agree with Molther. "I agreed with all he said of the power of faith," said Wesley. "But I could not agree either that none has any faith so long as he is liable to any doubt or fear; or, that till we have it, we ought to abstain from the Lord's Supper or the other ordinances of God."[6]

Wesley left a few days later for Oxford and Bristol but first urged the society members to use the means of grace.

While at Bristol and elsewhere Wesley received "several unpleasant accounts" of the situation at Fetter Lane. One wrote that "Brother Hutton, Clarke, Edmonds, and Bray are determined to go on according to Mr. Molther's directions, and to *raise a church*, as they term it; and I suppose above half our brethren are on their side."[7] Wesley returned to London on December 19 where he found "the dreadful effects of our brethren's reasoning and disputing with each other. Scarce one in ten retained his first love; and most of the rest were in the utmost confusion, biting and devouring one another."[8] On December 31 he had an unsatisfactory conference with Molther.

The story from Hutton's and Molther's side highlights both the issues and the personalities involved in the dispute. Hutton wrote to Count Zinzendorf on March 14:

J. Wesley being resolved to do *all things himself, and having told many souls that they were justified, who have since discovered themselves to be otherwise; and having mixed the works of the law with the Gospel as* means *of grace, is at enmity against the Brethren.*

. . . I desired him simply to keep his office in the body of Christ, i.e. *namely, to awaken souls in preaching, but not to pretend to lead them to Christ. But he will have the glory of doing all things. I fear by and by he will be an open enemy of Christ and his Church. Charles Wesley is coming to London, and determined to oppose all such as shall not use the means of grace (after his sense of them); I am determined to be still—I will let our Saviour govern this whirlwind.*

. . . J. W. and C. W., both of them, are dangerous snares to many young women; several are in love with them. I wish they were once married to some good sisters, but I would not give them one of my sisters if I had many. [9]

Fortunately, Wesley ignored Hutton's advice "not to pretend to lead" people to Christ.

For his part, Molther writes:

The Society in Fetter Lane had been under the care of John and Charles Wesley. The good people, not knowing rightly what they wanted, had adopted many most extraordinary usages. The very first time I entered their meeting, I was alarmed and almost terror-stricken at hearing their sighing and groaning, their whining and howling, which strange proceeding they called the demonstration of the Spirit and of power. In the midst of it all, it was quite apparent, from conversation with individuals, that most of them, from the very depth of their hearts, were yearning for the salvation of their souls. [10]

Wesley's personal ministry in London was growing even as the Fetter Lane crisis deepened. For some time Wesley had been preaching to large crowds in Moorfields, a popular park and recreation area. Soon he needed a regular meeting place. Nearby stood the abandoned Royal Foundry, a former cannon factory but now a barren shell due to an explosion and fire thirty-three years earlier. Here Wesley saw an answer to his need for a building. At the end of 1739 he leased and remodeled the improbable hulk.[11] The first service was held there on November 11, 1739, and the building became his headquarters early in 1740.[12] By June the Methodist Society at the Foundry numbered 300 members.[13] Wesley was not about to be sidetracked, nor could he agree with Molther that he lacked true faith. As Ronald Knox observes in *Enthusiasm,* "While Molther and Hutton were trying to convince Wesley that the only way to attain true conversion was to wait for it in perfect stillness, he was preaching . . . to people who cried as in the agonies of death" and who were freed "then and there from the power of the devil. For Wesley, the experimentalist, it was enough."[14]

Wesley continued trying to wean the Fetter Lane folks from Molther's "stillness" doctrine. On January 1, 1740, he tried to explain to the society what "true stillness" really is. He was in Bristol, Oxford and elsewhere for most of January, March and April, but returned on April 22 because of the continuing confusion at Fetter Lane. He and Charles spent two hours with Molther on April 25 and met with the society to discuss the question of ordinances. After another prolonged stay in Bristol, Wesley returned again to London in early June. He met with the society several more times, but on the night of July 16, after extensive debate, Wesley saw the breach was beyond repair.

The final break occurred, ironically, at a Sunday evening love feast four days later. Asked not to speak further, Wesley read a short paper stating his points of disagreement with Molther. Then he and about eighteen of the sixty or so present walked out of the meeting. Lady Huntingdon, apparently, was one of those who left with the Wesleys.[15]

The following Wednesday, Wesley notes, "Our little company met at *The Foundery,* instead of Fetter Lane." About twenty-five persons were present.[16] Wesley henceforth was to work independently of the Moravians. For its part, the Fetter Lane Society gradually evolved from July 1740 to October 1742 from an Anglican religious society into a Moravian congregation.[17] Molther went on to Pennsylvania, and in April 1741 Spangenberg was sent to organize and superintend Moravian work in England. In 1742 Spangenberg organized the seventy-some remaining members of the Fetter Lane Society into the first Moravian congregation in London.[18] Among the members were James Hutton, "the first English Moravian," who nevertheless remained on reasonably good terms with the Wesleys and continued publishing some of their books and hymns.[19]

What were Wesley's reasons for separating from the Fetter Lane Society? The Moravian historian Holmes attributes the breach to misunderstandings arising from language and cultural differences. Clearly these played some part, but much more was at stake. Molther's views were probably not totally representative of the Moravians at large, although Spangenberg seemed to agree with him.

Wesley always spoke highly of the Moravians in general, while criticizing particular points with which he could not agree. The immediate point of disagreement in 1740 was Wesley's insistence on the Anglican understanding of the means of grace. But Wesley had other objections as well. He wrote his brother Charles in April 1741:

As yet I dare in nowise join with the Moravians: 1. Because their whole scheme is mystical, not scriptural,–refined in every point above what is written, immeasurably beyond the plain doctrines of the Gospel. 2. Because there is darkness and closeness in all their behaviour, and guile in almost all their words. 3. Because they not only do not practise, but utterly despise and deny, self-denial and the daily cross. 4. Because they, upon principle, conform to the world, in wearing gold or costly apparel. 5. Because they extend Christian liberty, in this and many other respects, beyond what is warranted by holy writ. 6. Because they are by no means zealous of good works; or, at least, only to their own people. And, lastly, because they make inward religion swallow up outward in general. For these reasons chiefly I will rather, God being my helper, stand quite alone, than join with them: I mean, till I have full assurance that they will spread none of the errors among the little flock committed to my charge.[20]

In many ways this picture does not seem to fit the Moravian

colony at Herrnhut. Wesley is responding, rather, to the small band of Moravians he observed in London. This and other descriptions may hint at a marked socio-economic difference between these Moravians and Wesley's little flock at the Foundry.

Concerning the ordinances of God, Wesley felt Moravian practice was better than their principle. He thought the whole Moravian Church was "tainted with Quietism, Universal Salvation, and Antinomianism."[21] In regard to Molther Wesley said, "The great fault of the Moravian Church seems to lie in not openly disclaiming all he had said; which in all probability they would have done, had they not leaned to the same opinion."[22]

The Moravian Contribution The events from Wesley's return to England in 1738 to his separation from the Moravians in 1740 show that he both benefited from and reacted against the Moravians. The two great contributions to Wesley were in clarifying and leading him into the experience of saving faith, and in providing him models of Christian life-in-community. That he actually saw the Moravian Brethren as a model for renewal within the larger established church, as an *ecclesiola in ecclesia,* is questionable, for Wesley knew the Moravians had in fact become a separate church, despite Zinzendorf's vision. In accusing them of "guile" Wesley may have been questioning the sincerity of Moravian claims to be a renewing body within the churches rather than a separate church. The Pietist institutions at Halle may have appealed more to him as models of what could happen within the established church.

But Wesley was led to the existential meaning of salvation by faith through the Moravians, especially through Böhler and Spangenberg. From them he also learned how useful the religious society structure could be in nurturing heart religion and the value of smaller, more intimate "bands."

The more Wesley got to know the Moravians, the more he felt two distinctly different visions of the church were at stake. The Moravians were right to teach justification by faith and regeneration solely through the merits of the blood of the Lamb. But Wesley felt the Moravians were weak at two crucial points: They did not take seriously enough the sacramental side of the church, and their inward spirituality was not balanced by a proper emphasis on the ethical side of Christian life—disciplined living, good works and preaching the gospel to the poor. The life of Christian holiness as both an inward and an outward reality was still Wesley's goal. From the Moravians Wesley learned the inwardness of faith, but he insisted on balancing this with that stream of Anglican piety that insisted on holy living. Wesley was convinced this balance was biblical. Throughout his life he would insist that the biblical ideal was "faith working by love."

The striking thing about Wesley is that he was willing to go so far with the Moravians but no further. He was not at all ready to abandon the proper place of human agency in the plan of salvation. He saw that works were worthless in attaining the new birth, but he was equally persuaded of the absolute moral necessity of good works as the evidence of regeneration and the inevitable expression of holy love. Likewise, he could not be convinced that total dependence on God's grace required abandoning the *means* of grace. Wesley's conviction of the proper place of reason and his years of painstaking study of Christian antiquity (including the perfectionist teachings of fourth-century Eastern Fathers) kept him from becoming intellectually converted to all Moravian ideas after his spiritual conversion at Aldersgate. As Gerald Cragg states, "The Moravians had shown Wesley the true nature of saving faith; he was astonished that they seemed so blind to its necessary implications. Their Lutheran background made them recoil from anything suggestive of good works. Wesley believed that they were making the religious life a flight from responsibility."[23]

At issue here was the classical question of human cooperation in the work of salvation, the question of synergism.
Wesley objected to a rigid Calvinist position on this point,
adopting a somewhat more Arminian view. L. M. Starkey has
called Wesley's view an "evangelical synergism"—evangelical
because it is distinct "from other types which allow man a
natural capacity to co-operate with the divine spirit."[24] Wesley was very clear that salvation was wholly by grace alone.
But he was equally insistent that God graciously enabled men
and women to cooperate with the Holy Spirit in the great
work of salvation, of restoring the image of God. Therefore a
believer's failure to do his or her part in cooperating with
God's work was sheer disobedience. On this basis Wesley re-
sisted a number of Moravian tendencies and finally broke
with the Moravians.

At several significant points where Wesley reacted against
Moravianism he was moving in the direction of an older
Radical Protestantism, upholding a believers' church view in
opposition to Moravian-Pietist accommodations to Luther-
anism.

An interesting aspect here is the similarity in ecclesiology
between Wesley and Count Zinzendorf. Zinzendorf had
worked out a rather elaborate theory of the church and
church renewal based on an adaptation of the *ecclesiola in
ecclesia* idea. His "Tropus" theory saw the church in each
country as having something unique to contribute to the
universal church. He argued for the utility of movements
such as Moravianism as missionary and renewing structures
within the church. Like Wesley, Zinzendorf was a creative
and charismatic leader who sought to direct a burgeoning
movement toward a renewing impact on the whole church
rather than becoming a separate church. For these reasons Zinzendorf's ecclesiology is worthy of study in its own
right.

Beginning at the Foundry   By the time of his break with the Moravians Wesley was already employed full time in preaching, writing and organizing the growing Methodist work in London, Bristol and elsewhere. The Foundry became his headquarters, a beehive of activity. In remodeling the old structure Wesley had built a galleried chapel to hold 1,500 people, a large room which would accommodate 300, a dispensary and a bookroom for the sale of his books and pamphlets. Here he opened a free school for sixty children, a shelter for widows and the first free dispensary in London since the breakup of the monasteries.[25] Wesley put plain benches instead of pews in the chapel, noting that "all the benches for rich and poor were of the same construction."[26] How bold a move on Wesley's part this was can only be appreciated in light of the widespread eighteenth-century practice of purchasing one's own pew in church. Wesley had a set of rooms on the second floor. "I myself," he said, "as well as the other Preachers who are in town, diet with the poor, on the same food, and at the same table; and we rejoice herein, as a comfortable earnest of our eating bread together in our Father's kingdom."[27]

As the Methodist movement grew, as many as sixty-six class meetings met at the Foundry weekly. Two weekly prayer meetings were held, and Wesley or one of his preachers spoke daily at 5:00 a.m. "It was a settlement almost on the Franciscan model," comments Frederick Gill.[28] Or one may think of Augustine with his helpers and parishioners gathered around him in fourth-century Hippo.

Wesley's work at the Foundry shows his profound identification with the poor. This was, in fact, one of the points of criticism. An article in the June 1741 *Gentleman's Magazine* describing the meetings at the Foundry complained, "Most of those Persons, who frequent them, are the poorest and meanest Sort of People, who have families to provide for, and hardly Bread to put in their Mouths."[29] Maldwyn Edwards suggests that Wesley practically discovered the poor—"His life was one long crusade in the cause of the poor, and he encouraged others to follow his example."[30] Wesley had on the one hand a profound compassion for and interest in the poor, while on the other hand he distrusted the masses as a political force, convinced that government by the aristocracy was best.[31]

Wesley himself wrote, "I have found some of the uneducated poor, who have the most exquisite taste and sentiment, and many, very many of the rich who have scarcely any at all. In most genteel religious persons there is such a mixture that I scarcely ever have confidence in them; but I love the poor, and in many of them find pure genuine grace unmixed with folly and affectation. . . . If I might choose, I should still preach the gospel to the poor."[32]

No Turning Back By the late 1740s Methodism had set its course. "The People called Methodists" seemed to be everywhere. Wesley saw them as a renewing force within the Church of England, committed to proving in experience what the church professed in doctrine. They preached costly religion on the one hand, but also the universal offer of salvation on the other. When Whitefield began emphasizing his more rigid doctrine of election, Wesley turned away from him as decisively as he had from the Moravians. Methodism was the offer of God to all, but also the power of God for transformed living in all who believed.

These years were the making of John Wesley as a radical Christian. The direction had been set, the momentum established. With remarkably little variation Wesley worked tirelessly over the next fifty years to bring a radical reformation to the church. At every point of conflict he determined to be as radical as the Bible, to be faithful to "the law and the testimony" as he understood them.

By this time Wesley was largely disowned and ignored by

most in the established church. He continued however as a Fellow of Oxford University, which meant he was legally bound to preach before the University at least once every third year, and the University was required to hear him. Thus Wesley had preached at Oxford in 1738, 1741 and finally in 1744. These three sermons, as George Croft Cell notes, contrast with Wesley's sermons prior to 1738. "They are Revival manifestoes," boldly assailing "the dead theology and decadent Christianity of Oxford circles and of the Church at large."[33]

Wesley preached his last Oxford sermon, "Scriptural Christianity," on August 24. Tracing "scriptural Christianity" from the days after Pentecost and down through history, Wesley asked:

Where does this Christianity now exist? Where, I pray, do the Christians live? Which is the country, the inhabitants whereof are all thus filled with the Holy Ghost? are all of one heart and of one soul? cannot suffer one among them to lack anything, but continually give to every man as he hath need? who, one and all, have the love of God filling their hearts, and constraining them to love their neighbour as themselves? . . . who offend not in any kind, either by word or deed, against justice, mercy, or truth; but in every point do unto all men, as they would these should do unto them?[34]

Wesley made it plain he didn't believe such Christian faith was to be found at Oxford, and he called for repentance.

The reaction—and some measure of Wesley the man—can be gauged by the eyewitness report of twenty-five-year-old Benjamin Kennicott, later an eminent Hebrew scholar in England:

On Friday last, being St. Bartholomew's Day, the famous Methodist, Mr. John Wesley, Fellow of Lincoln College, preached before the University; which being a matter of great curiosity at present, and may possibly be greater in its consequences, I shall be particular in the account of it. All that are Masters of Arts, and on the foundation of any College, are set down in a roll, as they take their degree, and in that order preach before the University, or pay three guineas for a preacher in their stead, and as no clergyman can avoid his turn, so the University can refuse none; otherwise Mr. Wesley would not have preached. He came to Oxford some time before, and preached frequently every day in courts, public-houses, and elsewhere. On Friday morning, having held forth twice in private, at five and eight, he came to St. Mary's at ten o'clock. There were present the Vice-Chancellor, the proctors, most of the heads of houses, a vast number of gownsmen, and a multitude of private people, with many of his followers, both brethren and sisters, who, with funereal faces and plain attire, came from around to attend their master and teacher. When he mounted the pulpit, I fixed my eyes on him and his be-havior. He is neither tall nor fat; for the latter would ill become a Methodist. His black hair quite smooth, and parted very exactly, added to a peculiar composure in his countenance, showed him to be an un-common man. His prayer was soft, short, and conformable to the rules of the University. . . . he expressed himself like a very good scholar, but a rigid zealot; and then he came to what he called his plain, practical conclusion. Here was what he had been preparing for all along; and he fired his address with so much zeal and unbounded satire as quite spoiled what otherwise might have been turned to great advantage; for as I liked some, so I disliked other parts of his dis-course extremely. . . . I liked some of his freedom; such as calling the generality of young gownsmen "a generation of triflers," and many other just invectives. But, considering how many shining lights are here that are the glory of the Christian cause, his sacred censure was much too flaming and strong, and his charity much too weak in not making large allowances. But so far from allowances, that, after having summed up the measure of our iniquities, he concluded with a lifted-up eye in this most solemn form: "It is time for Thee, Lord, to lay to Thine hand"—words full of such presumption and seeming imprecation, that they gave an universal shock. This, and the assertion that Oxford was not a Christian city, and this country not a Chris-tian nation, were the most offensive parts of the sermon. . . . Had these things been omitted, and his censures moderated, I think his discourse, as to style and delivery, would have been uncommonly pleasing to others as well as to myself. He is allowed to be a man of great parts, and that by the excellent Dean of Christ Church; for the day he preached the dean generously said of him, "John Wesley will always be thought a man of sound sense, though an enthusiast." However, the Vice-Chancellor sent for the sermon and I hear the heads of colleges intend to show their resentment.[35]

Wesley was no longer welcome at Oxford, nor in most of the established churches of the day. He had broken with the Moravians. But the common people heard him gladly, and the people called Methodists were multiplying. Yet Wesley refused to turn his back on the Church of England. By skill and determination he not only formed the Methodist movement but steadfastly held it to its renewing mission within the established church.

5

NEW

WINESKINS

John Wesley saw that new wine must be put into new wine-skins. So the story of Wesley's life and ministry is the story of creating and adapting structures to serve the burgeoning revival movement.

The system which emerged gave lie to the argument that you can't build a church on poor and uneducated folk. Not only did Wesley reach the masses; he made leaders of thousands of them.

Within a few years of 1738 the Methodist system of societies, classes and bands, traveling preachers, simple preaching houses, and quarterly love feasts had been set up and was functioning well under Wesley's watchful eye. In chapter three we noted the origin of some of these forms. The Methodist structure needs closer scrutiny, however, because at one level it constitutes the genius of the whole movement, and at this point Wesley's understanding of "church" speaks forcefully to the present scene.

The emerging patterns composed, above all, a system of discipline-in-community. E. Douglass Bebb in his study of Wesley's social concern notes, "The Methodist church discipline of the eighteenth century has no parallel in modern English ecclesiastical history." It "would be regarded as intolerable by almost all members of any Christian communion in this country to-day."[1] The strictness of this discipline and its immersion in close koinonia will be evident as we look more carefully at the whole system.

Such discipline produced a rapidly growing body of earnest adherents. After thirty years, in 1768, Methodism had 40 circuits and 27,341 members. Ten years later the numbers had grown to 60 circuits and 40,089 members; in another decade, 99 circuits and 66,375 members. By 1798, seven years after Wesley's death, the totals had jumped to 149 circuits with 101,712 members. This is the stuff that church growth charts are made of! By the turn of the century about one in every thirty adult Englishmen were Methodists[2]— roughly proportionate to the strength of Methodism in the United States today.

The Class Meeting The Methodist societies were soon divided into classes and bands. Perhaps it would be more accurate to say the societies were the sum total of class and band members, since the primary point of belonging was this more intimate level of community and membership in a class was required before one could join the society. The system functioned much as does the "mission groups" structure today in the Church of the Savior in Washington, D. C.

The class meeting was the cornerstone of the whole edifice. The classes were in effect house churches (not classes for instruction, as the term *class* might suggest), meeting in the various neighborhoods where people lived. The class leaders (men and women) were pastors and disciplers. After the fortuitous organization of classes at Bristol the class sytem was introduced in London in 1742 and became the established Methodist pattern throughout England by 1746.[3]

The duties of the class leader as given by Wesley were twofold:

(1.) To see each person in his class, once a week at the least, in order

to inquire how their souls prosper; to advise, reprove, comfort, or exhort, as occasion may require; to receive what they are willing to give, toward the relief of the poor.

(2.) To meet the Minister and the Stewards of the society, in order to inform the Minister of any that are sick, or of any that are disorderly and will not be reproved; to pay the Stewards what they have received of their several classes in the week preceding.[4]

In his sermon "On God's Vineyard," Wesley later gave the following description of how the class meeting came to function as a key part of the Methodist system:

Any person determined to save his soul may be united (this is the only condition required) with them [the Methodists]. But this desire must be evidenced by three marks: Avoiding all known sin; doing good after his power; and, attending all the ordinances of God. He is then placed in such a class as is convenient for him, where he spends about an hour in a week. And, the next quarter, if nothing is objected to him, he is admitted into the society: And therein he may continue as long as he continues to meet his brethren, and walks according to his profession.[5]

The classes normally met one evening each week for an hour or so. Each person reported on his or her spiritual progress, or on particular needs or problems, and received the support and prayers of the others. "Advice or reproof was given as need required, quarrels were made up, misunderstandings removed: And after an hour or two spent in this labour of love, they concluded with prayer and thanksgiving."[6]

The class meeting became the backbone of the Methodist financial system as well. "A penny a week and a shilling a quarter" became the rule. The considerable sums thus raised and handled by the stewards were used for the poor and later provided the main support for the Methodist traveling preachers.[7]

Wesley argued for the class meeting on pragmatic and biblical grounds. "There is something not easily explained in the fellowship of the Spirit, which we enjoy in a society of living Christians," he noted.[8] He did not claim the class meeting was prescribed in Scripture but saw it as a prudential means of grace consistent with Scripture. He would have agreed with Henry Fish who later was to write one of the early manuals for class leaders. Fish pointed to Scriptures which yet today, in the twentieth century, often touch diseased areas in the body of Christ:

It is clear as daylight that that kind of communion [experienced in class meetings] has the express warrant of Holy Scripture; and that something more than Church communion in the sacrament of the Lord's supper was enjoyed by the primitive Christians. They had "fellowship," as well as "breaking of bread." How, for instance, could they exhort one another daily? How could they comfort and edify one another? How could they provoke one another to love and good works? How could they confess their faults to one another, and pray for one another? How teach and admonish one another in psalms, and hymns, and spiritual songs? How bear one another's burdens? How weep with those who weep, and rejoice with those who rejoice, if they never meet together for the purpose of conversing on experimental religion, and the state of each other's souls? Whatever persons may say to the contrary, those churches, the members of which do not observe, or in which they have not the opportunity of observing, the foregoing precepts which are enjoined in the New Testament Scriptures, are not based on the model of the apostolic Churches.[9]

The class meetings made such pointed biblical exhortations real in the lives of the Methodist people. The class meeting became the primary means of grace for thousands of Methodists. It served an evangelistic and discipling function. Wesley "wisely discerned that the beginnings of faith in a man's heart could be incubated into saving faith more effectively in the warm Christian atmosphere of the society than in the chill of the world."[10] According to one author it was, in fact, in the class meeting "where the great majority of conversions occurred."[11] The class meeting system tied together the widely scattered Methodist people and became the sustainer of the Methodist renewal over many decades. The movement was in fact a whole series of sporadic and often geographically localized revivals which were interconnected and spread by the society and class network, rather than one continuous wave of revival which swept the country. Without the class meeting, the scattered fires of renewal would have burned out long before the movement was able to make a deep impact on the nation.

It is easy to see how effective discipline could be exercised in such small groups when each person was known intimately by the class leader. As part of the system Wesley issued small cards or tickets to each class member. The card bore the person's name, the date and the signature of Wesley or one of his preachers. It was the member's proof of membership and admitted him or her to the quarterly love feast. Thus it was primarily membership in the *class* that constituted membership in the Methodist *society*, not vice versa. Unfaithful members didn't get their tickets renewed for the next quarter and thus were excluded from the feast. Wesley understood these tickets in the early Christian sense of letters of commendation.[12]

Wesley did not permit discipline to grow lax. In his periodic visits to the various places he "examined," "regulated" or "purged" the classes and societies as need required. He (or later his assistants) would carefully explain the rules and exclude any who were not seeking to follow them. Excluded members would then receive no quarterly membership tickets. Many of these would later be readmitted if they mended their ways.

Some examples show the extent of the discipline and the nature of the offenses. In 1748 Wesley reduced the Bristol society from 900 to 730, while on other occasions he found no expulsions were necessary. In port cities he often had to exclude some for smuggling and found with time that this discipline bore fruit in reduced smuggling in the area. From one society he expelled sixty-four persons, two for cursing, two for habitual Sabbath breaking, seventeen for drunkenness, two for selling liquor, three for quarreling, one for wife beating, three for habitual lying, four for evil speaking, one for idleness, and twenty-nine for "lightness and carelessness."[13] Bebb notes, "Few were expelled for strictly religious faults, and none for doctrinal differences, while significantly enough, the largest number were excluded for not taking seriously enough their religion, and to take it seriously always involved, in Wesley's view, right conduct to one's neighbour."[14] In exercising discipline "the question is not," said Wesley, "concerning the heart, but the life. And the general tenor of this . . . cannot be hidden without a miracle."[15] Therefore discipline was both possible and necessary.

The pastoral role of the class leaders with their little flocks of a dozen or so was especially important. Wesley's appointed lay preachers were constantly on the move from place to place, and in most cases the Anglican clergy took no responsibility for the pastoral care of the Methodists. The rapid growth of Methodism could never have occurred without the traveling preachers. But, Methodist historian Abel Stevens notes, these preachers "could never have secured the moral discipline, or even the permanence of its societies, without the pastoral care of the Class-leader, in the absence of the pastor, who at first was scarcely a day at a time in any one place."[16]

Class leaders were not, however, merely a makeshift arrangement so the Methodist societies could get by without full-time pastors. Rather the class leaders were, in a fundamental sense, themselves pastors. This was the normal system, based in part on Wesley's conviction that spiritual oversight had to be intimate and personal and that plural leadership was the norm in a congregation. He could never be convinced that it "was ever the will of the Lord that any congregation should have one teacher only." "This preacher has one talent, that another," he said. "No one whom I ever yet knew has all the talents which are needful for beginning, continuing, and perfecting the work of grace in a whole congregation."[17] This is part of the reason the Methodist preachers traveled on circuits. What one preacher lacked, the next one might supply.

The Band System   The classes were buttressed by the bands which, like those in Herrnhut, were smaller and generally divided by age, sex and marital status. Among the Moravians the bands were an ancient tradition, tracing back well before Zinzendorf's time.[18] Wesley followed the Moravian system but with some modifications. In particular he dropped the Moravian pattern of band "monitors" whose job it was to report on and exhort those who needed spiritual help or appeared to be in error. Wesley felt this undercut the mutual responsibility of each member to the others in the band.[19]

Band members were expected to abstain from doing evil, to be zealous in good works, including giving to the poor, and to use all the means of grace. Wesley drew up the following statement of rules:

The design of our meeting is, to obey that command of God, "Confess your faults one to another, and pray for one another, that ye may be healed."

To this end, we intend,—

1. To meet once a week, at the least.

2. To come punctually at the hour appointed, without some extraordinary reason.

3. To begin (those of us who are present) exactly at the hour, with singing or prayer.

4. To speak each of us in order, freely and plainly, the true state of our souls, with the faults we have committed in thought, word, or deed, and the temptations we have felt, since our last meeting.

5. *To end every meeting with prayer, suited to the state of each person present.*

6. *To desire some person among us to speak his own state first, and then to ask the rest, in order, as many and as searching questions as may be, concerning their state, sins, and temptations.*[20]

Questions to be asked each week were: (1) What known sins have you committed since our last meeting? (2) What temptations have you met with? (3) How were you delivered? (4) What have you thought, said, or done, of which you doubt whether it be sin or not?[21]

The bands caused some suspicion and the charge of "popery" because of the practice of confession. But they proved to be a useful means of spiritual growth. Unlike the classes, the bands were not mainly disciplinary but were to aid the spiritual progress of those who were clearly converted. Normally they averaged between five and ten persons in size.

The bands, unlike the classes, were restricted to persons who had the assurance of the remission of sins. Wesley's traveling preachers or assistants were to "closely examine" every band member and to "put out two in three, if they find so many in the best of their judgment, Unbelievers."[22] Band tickets were issued quarterly to all band members. These differed from the class or society tickets in various ways, sometimes by the printed word *BAND* or the letter *b* on the face of the ticket. These tickets functioned much as did the class tickets and admitted the bearers to the love feasts, covenant services and society meetings.[23]

Understandably, with this kind of rigor fewer bands were organized than classes. Judging from the number of band and class tickets printed, it would appear that about twenty per cent of the Methodist people met in bands, whereas all were class members.[24] Since the bands averaged about six members and the classes about twelve, this means there were probably about two or three classes for every band.

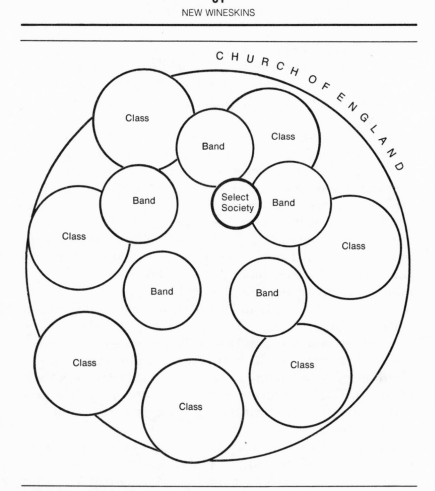

THE METHODIST SYSTEM
Under John Wesley

Wesley provided an even more intimate cell group, the Select Society, for those who appeared to be making marked progress toward inward and outward holiness, and also instituted separate groups for penitents. These group structures were all functioning by 1744. Thus Wesley explained in the 1744 Conference Minutes that the "United Societies," divided into classes, "consist of awakened persons. Part of these, who are supposed to have remission of sins, are more closely united in the Bands. Those in the Bands, who seem to walk in the light of God, compose the Select Societies. Those of them who have made shipwreck of the faith, meet apart as penitents."[25]

Wesley laid down three rules beyond the band rules for the Select Societies: "1. Let nothing spoken in this Society be spoken again; no, not even to the members of it. 2. Every member agrees absolutely to submit to his Minister in all indifferent things. 3. Every member, till we can have all things common, will bring once a week, *bona fide*, all he can spare towards a common stock."[26] The reference to "all things common" suggests that at this stage Wesley held the ideal of a true community of goods among those who were closest to attaining the life of the Kingdom of God.[27]

The system of bands and classes instituted by Wesley continued for over a century. In England the bands disappeared about 1880 (the last band tickets were issued that year[28]), while class meetings in both England and America survived into the twentieth century, at least in some Methodist churches. One still meets people who attribute their conversion or spiritual nurture to early experience in a Methodist class meeting.

Well before 1900 the class system had lost its vitality, however, in most of Methodism. Where it survived, the classes often became legalistic or moralistic; the life had long since departed. Among British Methodists class attendance was a condition of church membership until 1912, while in the United States the Methodist Episcopal Church, South dropped the requirement in 1866. A spate of books and some conventions attempted to revive the class meetings in America after 1850, but without success.[29]

Pastors and Leaders The society-class-band system would not have held together had it not been for "the itineracy"—

Wesley's system of traveling lay preachers. These preachers were under Wesley's direct supervision. If Methodism in general looked like a quasi-monastic order, the itineracy was *in fact* an order—a preaching order which, if not celibate, certainly knew about poverty and obedience. "The itinerants were taught to manage difficulties in the societies, to face mobs, to brave any weather, to subsist without means, except such as might casually occur on their routes, to rise at four and preach at five o'clock, to scatter books and tracts, to live by rule, and to die without fear."[30] The amazing thing was that they did so! Wesley gave them strict rules, expecting them to preach, study, travel, meet with bands and classes, exercise daily and eat sparingly.

The extensive system of bands, classes, societies and preachers, together with other offices and functions, opened the doors wide for leadership and discipleship in early Methodism. By the time Methodism had reached 100,000 members at the end of the century, the movement must have had over 10,000 class and band leaders with perhaps an equal or larger total of other leaders. Many of these, as well as some of Wesley's preachers, were women, prompting Bebb to call Wesley "the most outstanding feminist of the eighteenth century" because he provided women with opportunities for leadership available nowhere else.[31]

Now here is a remarkable thing. One hears today that it is hard to find enough leaders for small groups or the other responsibilities in the church. Wesley put one in ten, perhaps one in five, to work in significant ministry and leadership. And who were these people? Not the educated or the wealthy with time on their hands, but laboring men and women, husbands and wives and young folks with little or no training, but with spiritual gifts and eagerness to serve. Community became the incubator and training camp for Christlike ministry.

All of this provoked some disdain and mockery from Wesley's critics. Augustus Toplady, for instance, author of "Rock of Ages," accused Wesley's lay preaching system of "prostituting the ministerial function to the lowest and most illiterate mechanics, persons of almost any class, but especially common soldiers, who pretended to be pregnant with 'a message from the Lord.' " His advice for Wesley: "Let his cobblers keep to their stalls. Let his tinkers mend their vessels. Let his barbers confine themselves to their blocks and basons. Let his bakers stand to their kneading-troughs. Let his blacksmiths blow more suitable coals than those of controversy."[32]

Wesley saw, however, that such folk were the stuff true saints and ministers were made of.

Such was the Methodist system, built, adjusted and closely monitored by John Wesley. Wesley saw the world as his parish, but he "refused to preach in any place where he could not follow it up by organized Societies with adequate leadership."[33] He was out to make disciples—disciples who would renew the whole church.

two

RETHINKING
THE CHURCH

6

WHAT IS
THE CHURCH?

John Wesley knew what he was doing. He was sufficiently steeped in church history and Anglican ecclesiology to understand that the concept of the church was at stake in his reforming mission. From early in his ministry he pondered basic questions as to the nature, form and function of the Christian church.

The major sources of Wesley's ecclesiology were the Catholic tradition mediated through Anglicanism and the Radical Protestant tradition mediated mainly through the Moravian Brethren. Perhaps it would be more accurate to say his views on the church were essentially those of seventeenth-century Anglicanism, but interpreted in such a way as to conform to the believers' church understanding of the Christian community. There were, of course, other tributary streams of influence such as Puritanism.

Wesley's first conscious consideration of ecclesiological questions can be traced to the years 1725-28, when he began in earnest his quest for inward holiness. His reading for ordination would have introduced him to three important themes: the life of holiness, the importance of the sacraments and the authority of the tradition of the primitive church. He accepted these views wholeheartedly, all of which were matters of ecclesiology as much as of soteriology.

Baker notes that Wesley "firmly accepted the *via media* of the Church of England as incorporated in Cranmer's *Book of Common Prayer,* and expounded in turn by Jewel as the fulfillment of Scripture and the Fathers and by Hooker as the crown of human reasoning."[1] The Church of England—which Wesley always considered, overall, the best church in Christendom—was the middle way between Catholicism and Protestantism. John Jewel (1522-71) and Richard Hooker (ca. 1553-1600) had defended the Church of England against both Rome and extreme Puritanism, arguing that the Anglican Church was most compatible with Scripture and reason.[2]

Albert Outler summarizes the principal points of Jewel's ecclesiology, as presented in his *Apologia pro ecclesia Anglicana* (1562), under five heads:

1. The church's subordination to Scripture
2. The church's unity in Christ and the essentials of doctrine
3. The notion that paradigmata for ecclesiology should be drawn from the patristic age
4. The apostolic doctrine
5. The idea of a *functional* episcopacy (as belonging to the church's well-being rather than its essence).[3]

All these strands were woven permanently into Wesley's view of the church.

Development of Wesley's Views   Wesley examined questions of ecclesiology during his stay in Georgia. With his strong, practical reforming bent, he was especially interested in church order. Confronting a missionary situation brought these questions into focus with new urgency.

Wesley's father had urged him to read the sermons of Bishop William Beveridge (1637-1708) as being "perhaps as like those of the apostolical ages as any between them and us."[4] Beveridge, like Jeremy Taylor, was one of the "non-jurors" who refused to take the oath to William and Mary in 1689 and emphasized a life of deep devotion and sacramental piety. While in Georgia Wesley read Beveridge's *Synodikon*, a compilation of canons or regulations from early Greek councils which included the so-called *Apostolic Canons*. This reading, according to Baker, convinced Wesley of two things: that he had put too much stake in church tradition compared with Scripture, since some council decisions went beyond the Bible; and that consequently the foundation on which he had been building his ecclesiology was unsound.[5] Wesley had previously put great stock in the *Apostolic Canons*, but Beveridge convinced him that these were not as ancient or authentic as he had assumed. This meant Scripture and tradition were not an unbroken line, but that the two were sometimes in conflict. And, in case of conflict, tradition must give way. This was a radically new insight for Wesley.

Wesley continued to investigate matters of church order throughout his stay in Georgia. He delved into the question of episcopacy, the validity of Moravian orders and "lay baptism" (baptism by unordained ministers).[6] His study led him gradually to see church order more as a relative and less as an absolute matter. He discovered that many forms and practices had grown up through accumulated ecclesiastical tradition with no real biblical basis. But he felt matters of order and structure were very important. Already he had a keen sense of the place of structures and forms in Christian life and the life of the church.

Back in England, Wesley continued to move toward a more functional view of church order—without, however, departing from Anglican views, which ranged over a broad spectrum. Baker notes, "Already by 1746 Wesley saw the essence of the church and its ministry as functional rather than institutional."[7] Similarly, Robert Monk observes: "Wesley was willing rather early in his evangelical career to recognize the validity of various forms of church order. This recognition was not, however, foreign to Anglican divines either in Wesley's own time or during the preceding two centuries."[8]

Though Wesley was unsympathetic to the views of the so-called Latitudinarians on most points, it was two Latitudinarian writers who led him further toward a more functional view of the church. In 1746 Wesley read Lord Peter King's *Account of the Primitive Church*[9] and, about the same time, Edward Stillingfleet's *Irenicon*.[10] According to Baker, these books continued the "slow transformation" in Wesley's views on the church which was already happening due to Wesley's other reading and especially his personal faith and growing ministry as evangelist and pastor.[11] Wesley himself wrote, "I still believe 'the episcopal form of church government to be both scriptural and apostolical': I mean, well agreeing with the practice and writings of the apostles. But that it is *prescribed* in Scripture I do not believe. This opinion, which I once heartily espoused, I have been heartily ashamed of ever since I read Bishop Stillingfleet's *Irenicon*. I think he has unanswerably proved that 'neither Christ nor his apostles *prescribed* any particular form of church government, and that the plea of divine right for diocesan episcopacy was never heard of in the primitive church.' "[12]

These changes happened during the crucial first decade or so of Wesley's ministry following Aldersgate in 1738 and the beginning of field preaching in 1739. Wesley was soon appointing lay preachers, and the views of King and Stillingfleet confirmed him in the legitimacy of this move. Their arguments were to prove important later in the question of Wesley's right or authority to ordain ministers for America.

By 1750 Wesley was clear as to his basis of authority (in Baker's words): "the Anglican triad of Scripture, reason, and antiquity, strongly reinforced by an intuitive individualistic approach deriving in part both from Pietist and mystical influence. The appeal to reason, however, had developed into an urgent pragmatism."[13] The "Anglican triad" had, in fact, become "the Wesleyan quadrilateral" of Scripture, reason, tradition and *experience*, with Scripture as the "norming norm" to be placed above all other authority. Wesley was a man of reason in an age of rationalism; yet he was roundly charged with enthusiasm or fanaticism because of his stress on experience and his openness to the expression of emotion. He was at once a High Churchman and a Pietist; a traditionalist and an innovator; a biblicist and an experientialist. But he was always clear as to the priority of Scripture, especially from 1738 on, and his experiential emphasis was guarded from pure subjectivism not only by his respect for Scripture but also by his emphasis on the witness of the Spirit, the work of the Holy Spirit testifying to and confirming the Word in present experience.

Wesley's conception of the church grew out of this matrix.

Both Wesley's actions and his writings show that his ecclesiology combined two very different visions of the church. Frank Baker has noted this, commenting:

Throughout his adult life Wesley responded with varying degrees of enthusiasm to two fundamentally different views of the church. One was that of an historical institution, organically linked to the apostolic church by a succession of bishops and inherited customs, served by a priestly caste who duly expounded the Bible and administered the sacraments in such a way as to preserve the ancient traditions on behalf of all who were made members by baptism. According to the other view the church was a fellowship of believers who shared both the apostolic experience of God's living presence and also a desire to bring others into this same personal experience by whatever methods of worship and evangelism seemed most promising to those among them whom the Holy Spirit had endowed with special gifts of prophecy and leadership. The first view saw the church in essence as an ancient institution to be preserved, the second as a faithful few with a mission to the world: the first was a traditional rule, the second a living relationship.[14]

At one level these two views of the church look a lot like the distinction Ernst Troeltsch made between "church" and "sect." We might label them the institutional and charismatic perspectives. The question is, are these two perspectives mutually exclusive, or in some way complementary? This question and what it says for church life and renewal today will be investigated in some detail in chapter ten.

While Wesley never rejected either the institutional or the charismatic understanding of the church, his heart was with the latter. His lifelong mission was an effort to infuse the institutional church with the life of renewed Christian community.

Toward the end of his life, when he had already ordained leaders for American Methodism, Wesley published his sermons "Of the Church" and "On Schism." These show Wesley with essentially the same view of the church he had come to by 1750. To those who thought Wesley's actions were inconsistent with his profession of loyalty to the Church of England he responded:

They cannot but think so, unless they observe my two principles: The one, that I dare not separate from the Church, that I believe it would be a sin so to do; the other, that I believe it would be a sin not to vary from it in the points above mentioned. I say, put these two principles together, First, I will not separate from the Church; yet, Secondly, in cases of necessity, I will vary from it, (both of which I have constantly and openly avowed for upwards of fifty years,) and inconsistency vanishes away. I have been true to my profession from 1730 to this day. [15]

He was entirely consistent, Wesley said. "We act at all times on one plain uniform principle—we will obey the rulers and governors of the Church, whenever we can consistently with our duty to God, whenever we cannot, we will quietly obey God rather than men."[16]

Wesley could still say at the end of his life, "I am fully convinced that our own Church [of England], with all her blemishes, is nearer the scriptural plan than any other in Europe."[17]

What Is "Church"?   Wesley began his *Explanatory Notes on the New Testament* in 1743 and completed them in 1754, drawing on the work of the noted contemporary Pietist scholar J. A. Bengel. It is here Wesley gives some of his most succinct descriptions of the church.

The church is "the believers in Christ," "the whole body of Christian believers," "the whole body of true believers, whether on earth or in paradise."[18] Perhaps Wesley's comment on Acts 5:11 gives the clearest insight into his understanding of the New Testament church: "A company of men, called by the gospel, grafted into Christ by baptism, animated by love, united by all kind of fellowship, and disciplined by the death of Ananias and Sapphira."[19]

In his sermon "Of the Church" Wesley said the church is, in the proper sense, "a congregation, or body of people, united together in the service of God."[20] Even two or three united in Christ's name, or a Christian family, may therefore be called a church.[21] The primary expression of the church is the visible, gathered local congregation. But in a broader sense "church" means "the catholic or universal church; that is, all the Christians under heaven," understood as made up of all the local congregations in the world.[22] In "A Letter to a Roman Catholic" in 1749 Wesley said,

I believe that Christ by his Apostles gathered unto himself a Church, to which he has continually added such as shall be saved; that this catholic, that is, universal, Church, extending to all nations and all ages, is holy in all its members, who have fellowship with God the Father, Son and Holy Ghost; that they have fellowship with the holy angels, who constantly minister to these heirs of salvation; and with all the living members of Christ on earth, as well as all who are departed in his faith and fear.[23]

Wesley felt he could reconcile the New Testament understanding of the church with Article 19 of the Anglican Thirty-Nine Articles. He wrote,

A visible Church (as our Article defines it) is "a company of faithful (or believing) people: coetus credentium". *This is the essence of a Church, and the properties thereof are (as they are described in the words that follow), "that the pure word of God be preached therein, and the sacraments duly administered". Now, then, according to this authentic account, what is the Church of England? What is it, indeed, but the* faithful people, *the* true believers *of England? It is true, if these are scattered abroad they come under another consideration. But when they are visibly joined by assembling together to hear "the pure word of God preached" and to "eat of one bread" and "drink of one cup", they are then properly "the visible Church of England".*[24]

Wesley translated "faithful men" in the Article as "congregation of believers" on the basis of the Latin *coetus credentium;* actually the Latin version had *coetus fidelium.*[25] Wesley said he did not propose to defend this definition of the church, but he thought it was compatible with Scripture. Actually, he is straining here toward a more biblical and believers' church interpretation of what is primarily a rather institutional and sacramental formula, a formula going back to the Lutheran Augsburg Confession of 1530 and even before.[26]

The words in the Article "in which the pure word of God is preached, and the sacraments . . . duly administered" Wesley interpreted more functionally than formally. They meant that any congregation where the gospel was not truly preached or the sacraments not duly administered was neither a part of the Church of England nor of the universal church. Yet Wesley was charitable toward improper practices and even wrong doctrines if a congregation gave evidence of the Spirit's genuine presence:

Whoever they are that have "one Spirit, one hope, one Lord, one faith, one God and Father of all," I can easily bear with their holding wrong opinions, yea, and superstitious modes of worship; nor

would I, on these accounts, scruple still to include them within the pale of the catholic church; neither would I have any objection to receive them, if they desired it, as members of the Church of England.[27]

His sermon "Catholic Spirit" shows how far he was willing to go in recognizing different groups as genuinely belonging to the universal church:

We must both act as each is fully persuaded in his own mind. Hold you fast that which you believe is most acceptable to God, and I will do the same. I believe the Episcopal form of Church government to be scriptural and apostolical. If you think the Presbyterian or Independent is better, think so still, and act accordingly. I believe infants ought to be baptized; and that this may be done either by dipping or sprinkling. If you are otherwise persuaded, be so still, and follow your own persuasion. It appears to me, that forms of prayer are of excellent use, particularly in the great congregation. If you judge extemporary prayer to be of more use, act suitable to your own judgment. My sentiment is that I ought not to forbid water, wherein persons may be baptized; and that I ought to eat bread and drink wine, as a memorial of my dying Master: However, if you are not convinced of this, act according to the light you have. I have no desire to dispute with you one moment upon any of the preceding heads.[28]

Wesley could not have said such things had he not already decided that these questions do not touch the essence of the church. They were important questions but, finally, secondary. At heart, the church was the community of God's people.

Defining the church as a congregation of faithful believers does, however, point to some ambivalence and ambiguity, if not inconsistency, in Wesley. On the one hand the Church of England was essentially the "faithful people" or "true believers" visibly assembled together in Word and sacrament. But on the other hand Wesley virtually accused the Church of England of being apostate. There are only a few in England "whose inmost soul is renewed after the image of God," he wrote in 1763, "and as for a Christian *visible church,* or a body of Christians visibly united together, where is this to be seen?"[29]

Wesley considered the Church of England (and the whole Christian church generally) to be in a largely fallen state. In some formal sense the Church of England with its structures and liturgy was still a true church, but in fact and spirit the true church was really the small groups of faithful believers scattered throughout the Anglican and other communions.

Wesley seems to have seen the Methodist societies as comprising, to a large degree, the true visible church within Anglicanism. Yet as Methodism grew he recognized that not even all Methodists were "true believers" or "faithful men," and that as time went on this would be increasingly so.

Outler summarizes Wesley's mature understanding of the church (what he calls "the classical Methodist ecclesiology") as follows:

1. The unity *of the church is based upon the Christian* koinonia *in the Holy Spirit.*

2. The holiness *of the church is grounded in the discipline of grace which guides and matures the Christian life from its threshold in justifying faith to its [fullness] in sanctification.*

3. The catholicity *of the church is defined by the universal outreach of redemption, the essential community of all true believers.*

4. The apostolicity *of the church is gauged by the succession of apostolic doctrine in those who have been faithful to the apostolic witness.*[30]

This is an apt description. The church is *one* because "in all ages and nations it is the one body of Christ," endued with faith working by love.[31] Its *holiness* consists in the holiness of its members, "because every member thereof is holy, though in different degrees, as He that called them is holy";[32] "no unholy man can possibly be a member of it."[33] It is *catholic* because it is the people of God "dispersed over the whole earth, in Europe, Asia, Africa, and America."[34] And it is *apostolic,* for there has been an uninterrupted apostolic witness to the gospel through a faithful community and faithful ministers down through history.[35]

7
THE CHURCH
IN HISTORY

The church is a social and historical reality. It has a history—past, present, future. The Bible, a historical book, shows how God has worked in history. Nothing clarifies how we really understand the church like asking how the church functions in history.

Wesley's reading on the early church brought him, as noted earlier, to a more functional view of church order. But it also changed his thinking about church history. His concept of the church emerges more clearly when linked to his view of the church in history.

Wesley's reading in Georgia changed the direction of his strong primitivism. Beveridge's *Synodikon* undermined his faith in the apostolic origin and universal use of many church traditions. He now saw that antiquity should be no more than a "subordinate rule with scripture," rather than a coordinate rule, and that the period of the church's early faithfulness could not be extended, as he had before thought, into the fourth century.[1] For Anglicans, the "early church" meant the church of the first three or four centuries, while "primitive church" denoted the church of the New Testament period. Wesley increasingly focused upon the primitive church, especially after Aldersgate, less for its forms of order than for its spirit and corporate experience.[2]

A Fallen Church   Wesley came to agree with the German historian Gottfried Arnold (1666-1714) that the church had early fallen into unfaithfulness. According to Donald Durnbaugh, Wesley took a copy of Arnold's *True Portrayal of the First Christians* (1696) with him to Georgia and had read William Cave, one of Arnold's principal sources.[3] It is uncertain how much or how directly Arnold may have influenced Wesley, but the link with Arnold is suggestive since his writings were influential among eighteenth-century Mennonites and Brethren.[4] Franklin Littell notes that Arnold accepted "a very large share of the primitivist interpretation of Christian history which the Anabaptists had defended in the previous century."[5]

Wesley was later to speak in strong terms of the unfaithfulness of the church throughout history. In his sermon "The Mystery of Iniquity" he said:

Persecution never did, never could, give any lasting wound to genuine Christianity. But the greatest it ever received, the grand blow which was struck at the very root of that humble, gentle, patient love, which is the fulfilling of the Christian law, the whole essence of true religion, was struck in the fourth century by Constantine the Great, when he called himself a Christian, and poured in a flood of riches, honours, and power, upon the Christians; more especially upon the Clergy. . . . Just so, when the fear of persecution was removed, and wealth and honour attended the Christian profession, the Christians "did not gradually sink, but rushed headlong into all manner of vices." Then "the mystery of iniquity" was no more hid, but stalked abroad in the face of the sun. Then, not the golden age but the iron age of the church commenced. . . .

And this is the event which most Christian expositors mention with such triumph! yea, which some of them suppose to be typified in the Revelation, by "the New Jerusalem coming down from heaven!" Rather say, it was the coming of Satan and all his legions from the bottomless pit: seeing from that very time he hath set up his throne over the face of the whole earth, and reigned over the Christian as well as the Pagan world with hardly any control! . . . Such has been the deplorable state of the Christian church, from the time of Constantine till the Reformation. A Christian nation, a Christian city (according to the scriptural model), was nowhere to be seen; but every city and country, a few individuals excepted, was plunged in all manner of wickedness.[6]

And Wesley went on to say that the same fallen condition had, in large measure, continued right up to his day.

With this perspective on church history, Wesley looked sympathetically on second-century Montanism which he saw as somewhat parallel to Methodism. In the same sermon on the "Mystery of Iniquity" he said, "As to the heresies fathered upon Montanus, it is not easy to find what they were. I believe his grand heresy was, the maintaining that 'without' inward and outward 'holiness no man shall see the Lord.' "[7] In a brief piece on "The Real Character of Montanus" Wesley argued that, far from being a heretic, Montanus was "one of the best men then upon earth" who, "under the character of a Prophet, as an order established in the Church, appeared (without bringing any new doctrine) for reviving what was decayed, and reforming what might be amiss."[8] Apparently Wesley saw a parallel between Montanus and himself.

Wesley believed the Church of England as he knew it was as fallen as was Christianity generally. In 1745 he published "A Farther Appeal to Men of Reason and Religion," detailing the fallen state of the church and the nation of England.[9]

With such views, Wesley understandably gave a different interpretation to "Apostolic succession" than that commonly accepted in Anglicanism. By 1747 he came to believe that Anglican bishops were not in unbroken succession from the Apostles.[10] He wrote in 1761, "I deny that the Romish bishops came down by *uninterrupted* succession from the apostles. I never could see it proved; and, I am persuaded, I never shall."[11] True apostolic succession came to mean, therefore, the continuity of apostolic witness and spirit in the Christian community.

Wesley's view on the fallenness of the church could imply a rather negative and escapist outlook toward the church and its future in the world, such as found, for example, in modern premillennialism. But Wesley's confidence in the present working of grace gave him a dynamic and positive conviction concerning what God could accomplish through his people in the present order. Toward the end of his life, in his sermon "Of Former Times," he denied that the world is only getting worse and conditions were generally better in the past. "It is generally supposed, that we now live in the dregs of time," he noted, "and, consequently, that everything is in a declining state." But in fact "the former days were not better than these; yea, on the contrary, . . . these are in many respects, beyond comparison better than them." Wesley saw his day as an age of increased knowledge and toleration, much better than the days following the Reformation when many people were reformed merely in their "religious opinions . . . and modes of worship" but not in their daily lives.[12]

Looking back over the history of the church, Wesley concluded that except for the days immediately following Pentecost, the present time was the best so far. Even in the first century the "mystery of iniquity" began to work in the church, culminating with the baptism of the Emperor Constantine, "productive of more evil to the Church than all the ten persecutions put together." For at that time "the Church and State, the kingdoms of Christ and of the world, were so strangely and unnaturally blended together, . . . that they will hardly ever be divided till Christ comes to reign upon earth."[13]

In contrast, Wesley saw God's grace remarkably at work in his own time. "Benevolence and compassion toward all the forms of human woe have increased in a manner not known before," with the erection of many new hospitals, infirmaries and "other places of public charity." And then there was the particular phenomenon of Methodism, of which Wesley noted with pride:

I cannot forbear mentioning one instance more of the goodness of God to us in the present age. He has lifted up his standard in our islands, both against luxury, profaneness, and vice of every kind. He caused, near fifty years ago, as it were, a grain of mustard-seed to be sown near London; and it has now grown and put forth great branches, reaching from sea to sea. Two or three poor people met together, in order to help each other to be real Christians. They increased to hundreds, to thousands, to myriads, still pursuing their one point, real religion; the love of God and man ruling all their tempers, and words, and actions. Now I will be bold to say, such an event as this, considered in all its circumstances, has not been seen upon earth before, since the time that St. John went to Abraham's bosom.[14]

Wesley concluded that no time since the Apostolic age had been better than the present. "We are not born out of due time, but in the day of his power,—a day of glorious salvation, wherein he is hastening to renew the whole race of mankind in righteousness and true holiness."[15]

This dialectic between the fallenness of the church and the renewing work of the Spirit was basic to Wesley's outlook. It kept him from extreme pessimism or naive optimism, for his view was grounded, not in "progress" or the goodness and wisdom of people, but in the universal mercy and grace of God.

Wesley wrote in 1747, "I desire to have both heaven and hell ever in my eye, while I stand on this isthmus of life, between these two boundless oceans; and I verily think the daily consideration of both highly becomes all men of reason and religion."[16] Wesley lived the present in the light of the future. For him, that meant doing the work of the Kingdom of God here and now, as well as preparing for eternity.

The Possibilities of Grace   Wesley saw no necessary bounds to the free grace of God. He was fundamentally hopeful about the possibilities of God's grace working *now,* in the present, both in individuals and in society. He saw the whole work of salvation, and even creation, as an expression of God's grace. No person is so totally depraved, Wesley taught, as to be outside the grace of God. He wrote, "There is no man that is in a state of mere nature; there is no man, unless he has quenched the Spirit, that is wholly void of the grace of God."[17]

Wesley's emphasis on holiness must be seen in this light. He did not teach "sinless perfection," but he did teach that love could, and must, become the primary motivating force in the Christian's life. He repeatedly defined holiness as loving God with all one's being and loving one's neighbor as oneself. This meant two things for Wesley: God's grace was sufficient to perfect the Christian in love, and this love empowered and impelled the believer to good works. We must give ourselves to God in faith and "in holy, active, patient love."[18]

Wesley's emphasis on grace and on final judgment gave him a dynamic, rather than static, view of redemption. Salvation included sanctification, which included good works, "faith working by love." By God's grace, men and women were colaborers with God in the present work of redemption. Wesley saw the present order as an active battle between the kingdom of darkness and the Kingdom of God. Christians were not saved *out of* this battle, but were rather *called into it* to wrestle with principalities and powers. The Christian life is lived in the light of eternity—actively, not passively.

The hundreds of little Methodist societies which Wesley formed might almost be called "eschatological communities." Only one condition was required to join them: a desire "to flee from the wrath to come, to be saved from their sins." There was no doctrinal test, for Wesley was convinced that "a man may be orthodox in every point" and yet "have no religion at all."[19] Yet individuals could continue as Methodists only if they submitted to Methodist disciplines and lived lives of faith and good works. The church, said Wesley, is a "body of men compacted together, in order, first, to save each his own soul; then to assist each other in working out their salvation; and afterwards, as far as in them lies, to save all men from present and future misery, to overturn the kingdom of Satan, and set up the kingdom of Christ. And this ought to be the continued care and endeavour of every member of his church; otherwise he is not worthy to be called a member thereof, as he is not a living member of Christ."[20]

This perspective enabled Wesley, in thought and practice, to hold together three seeming antitheses which so often come unglued in the church. Since Wesley was more a gospel practitioner than a systematic theologian, his balance at these three points is visible as much in his practice as in his doctrine.

1. Wesley held together the eschatological hope and "the wrath to come." Often the church divides at this point, some Christians falling into a naive optimism while others preach hell and damnation. Wesley saw both emphases in Scripture, and both were part of his preaching. As A. Skevington Wood points out in *The Burning Heart,* judgment and "the terrors of the Lord" formed a frequent theme in Wesley's preaching. Wesley saw the preaching of judgment as "part of the awakening ministry which paves the way for the gospel offer."[21] He was optimistic about the possibilities of grace and emphatic that God would create a new heaven and a new earth. But this emphasis had to be combined with the warning of judgment and eternal punishment. Biblical realism required holding together eschatological hope and dread. Wood adds, "For Wesley the whole of life was visualized from the standpoint of the eternal. . . . His evangelistic mission was carried on in the knowledge . . . that both he and his hearers were living between the advents."[22]

2. Partly because of this, Wesley also held together the evangelistic and the prophetic dimensions of the gospel. There was no split between personal salvation and social engagement.

Wesley was first of all an evangelist. He felt that all must hear and respond to the convicting and converting Word of God. But the new birth must produce faith, hope and love, or else it was not true conversion. The "necessary fruit" of the love of God resulting from the new birth, said Wesley, is "the love of our neighbour; of every soul which God hath made." But this love is much more than a passive emotion; it involves "universal obedience to him we love, and conformity to his will. . . . And one of the tempers most obviously implied herein, is, the being 'zealous of good works;' the hungering and thirsting to do good, in every possible kind, unto all men; the rejoicing to 'spend and be spent for them,' for every child of man; not looking for any recompense in this world, but only in the resurrection of the just."[23]

Nowhere is this combination of the evangelistic and prophetic clearer than in Wesley's preaching to the poor. Wesley noted that preaching the gospel to the poor was a key proof of Jesus' messiahship and was "the greatest miracle of all." Jesus preached to those who were poor both "literally and spiritually."[24]

Migration to the cities had produced a new class of urban poor in Wesley's day. The Industrial Revolution was in full swing, fired by coal. When Wesley preached to the Kingswood colliers he was touching those most cruelly victimized by industrialization. Yet his response among the coal miners was phenomenal, and Wesley worked tirelessly for their spiritual and material welfare. Among other things, he opened free dispensaries, set up a kind of credit union, and established schools and orphanages. His ministry branched out to include lead miners, iron smelters, brass and copper workers, quarrymen, shipyard workers, farm laborers, prisoners and women industrial workers.

To all these people—the victims of society—Wesley offered the Good News of Jesus Christ. But he did more. He formed them into close-knit fellowships where they could be shepherded and where leaders could be developed, and he worked to reform the conditions under which they lived. His efforts went beyond welfare to include creative economic alternatives. Through his pointed and prolific writings he agitated for major reforms. He was convinced that "the making an open stand against all the ungodliness and unrighteousness which overspreads our land as a flood, is one of the noblest ways of confessing Christ in the face of His enemies."[25]

3. Finally, Wesley held in creative tension the present and future dimensions of salvation. The new birth began a process that reached into eternity. He reasoned that if God could make men and women holy in heaven, he could also make them holy on earth. His action for social welfare and reform ran parallel to this: God's grace is sufficient, and the power of love in believers is potent enough, to bring substantial improvement in social and economic conditions in the present age.

Wesley was not much concerned about eschatological roadmapping, and to the extent that he dealt with end-time events he largely took over the views of Bengel and others. As Wood points out, Wesley "confined himself to the bold outlines of prophecy, rather than wrestling with the details of debatable interpretation."[26] His view of Christ's Second Coming was postmillennial, but he did not emphasize the point. His primary focus was much more on the present operation of God's grace and love in believers in the light of the certainty of final judgment and of the "new heavens and new earth."

Wesley's concern for personal holiness has sometimes been distorted over the course of two hundred years, and its ethical and social dimensions have often been eclipsed. He was convinced that the social implications of holy living were inescapable. Thus he opposed mysticism and "solitary religion," arguing that "Holy solitaries," or, as we would say, solitary saints, "is a phrase no more consistent with the gospel than holy adulterers. The gospel of Christ knows of no religion, but social; no holiness but social holiness. 'Faith working by love' is the length and breadth and depth and height of Christian perfection."[27]

Faith Working by Love Love was the key dynamic in Wesley's whole life and theology. The Christian's life was to be one of active faith—faith working by love. For Wesley, the "pressure of the future" consisted in a combination of eschatological hope and dread permeated by love. Justice and righteousness were the outworking of love. He said, "Righteousness is the fruit of God's reigning in the heart. And what is righteousness, but love?—the love of God and of all mankind, flowing from faith in Jesus Christ, and producing humbleness of mind, meekness, gentleness, longsuffering, patience, deadness to the world; and every right disposition of heart, toward God and toward man. And by these it produces all holy actions, whatsoever are lovely or of good report; whatsoever works of faith and labour of love are acceptable to God, and profitable to man."[28]

Salvation for Wesley was a dynamic triad of faith, hope and love. Human beings could and must be colaborers with God in the great work of redemption. The work of the Spirit in Christians' lives would produce "holiness and happiness"[29] for them and for all who would respond in faith to God's gracious offer of salvation. But above and beyond all stood God in his sovereignty and the certainty of final judgment.

Preaching before assembled judges, officials and attendants at Bedford in 1758, Wesley spoke on "The Great Assize" —the Last Judgment. He assured his hearers of the final outcome of history: "And then only when God hath brought to light all the hidden things of darkness, whosoever were the actors therein, will it be seen that wise and good were all his ways; that he saw through the thick cloud, and governed all things by the wise counsel of his own will; that nothing was left to chance or the caprice of men, but God disposed all strongly and sweetly, and wrought all into one connected chain of justice, mercy, and truth."[30]

Wesley did not pluck the church out of history and plant it prematurely in heaven. Neither did he sanctify all the traditions and structures arrayed under the name "church." He saw the fallenness of the church, but also that it was still a channel of God's grace. He granted some value and function to the institutional church, even in its fallenness. But he worked ceaselessly for a more vital, more aggressive, more loving, and more authentically visible manifestation of the church as the community of God's people, the eschatological community which was to be the agent *now* of the coming Kingdom of God.

8

MINISTRY
AND SACRAMENT

Wesley's concern with reform and experience naturally led to the question of how and through whom the church ministers God's grace. So we find that Wesley's view of the church and its history carried over into matters of church order, ministry, ordination and the sacraments.

The question of orders of ministry arose when Wesley began appointing assistants to help Charles and himself in the work of preaching. How was this new body of preachers, most of whom were unordained, to be understood ecclesiologically? In what sense were they ministers? What authority did they have? And what was the meaning of Wesley's act of appointing them? These were inevitable and crucial questions given the rather specific theories and procedures of ordination and ministry within the Church of England.

The Wesleys themselves could claim authority to preach based on their Anglican ordination. Their only problem was to justify their unorthodox practice of field preaching and preaching indiscriminately across England, rather than staying put in one parish. John Wesley justified his itinerant ministry on at least two grounds: his Oxford fellowship gave him license to teach anywhere, and the results themselves justified his actions. "I did far more good," he remarked, "by preaching three days on my father's tomb than I did by preaching three years in his pulpit."[1] To critics who said he should stay in one parish only, he responded: "I look upon all the world as my parish; thus far I mean, that in whatever part of it I am I judge it meet, right, and my bounden duty to declare, unto all that are willing to hear, the glad tidings of salvation."[2]

But the case was different for Wesley's preachers, for they were unordained. What right did *they* have to preach, and what right did Wesley have to appoint them? Wesley had to face these questions.

Anglican Priests and Methodist Preachers   Here as elsewhere, Wesley's problem was to remain faithful to Scripture, the early church and the Church of England while moving to meet the ministry opportunities opening before him. How could he explain his ministry and his measures, not only to himself and to his critics, but also to his growing band of lay preachers?

Wesley insisted that he was appointing *preachers,* not *pastors,* and that his appointment was not ordination to the priesthood. Yet he saw his action as consistent with Anglican church order and with early church practice. Underlying his reasoning was, of course, his perception of the Methodist societies as an evangelical order within the Church of England, not as churches themselves.

Wesley thought he saw in Scripture and the early church a distinction between two kinds of Christian ministers—corresponding to the difference between Anglican priests and Methodist preachers—that would legitimize both. One order of ministers had responsibility to preach and evangelize; the other, to give pastoral care, administer the sacraments and ordain. Thus Wesley explained in his sermon, "The Ministerial Office,"

So the great High-Priest of our profession sent Apostles and Evan-

gelists to proclaim glad tidings to all the world; and then Pastors, Preachers, and Teachers, to build up in the faith the congregations that should be founded. But I do not find that ever the office of an Evangelist was the same with that of a Pastor, frequently called a Bishop. He presided over the flock, and administered the sacraments: The former assisted him, and preached the word, either in one or more congregations. I cannot prove from any part of the New Testament, or from any author of the three first centuries, that the office of an Evangelist gave any man a right to act as a Pastor or Bishop. I believe these offices were considered as quite distinct from each other till the time of Constantine.[3]

But with the fall of the church under Constantine, the situation was greatly altered:

It soon grew common for one man to take the whole charge of a congregation in order to engross the whole pay. Hence the same person acted as Priest and Prophet, as Pastor and Evangelist. And this gradually spread more and more throughout the whole Christian Church. Yet even at this day, although the same person usually discharges both these offices, yet the office of an Evangelist or Teacher does not imply that of a Pastor, to whom peculiarly belongs the administration of the sacraments.[4]

Applying this to the situation of Methodist preachers within the Church of England, Wesley saw his innovation as a return to New Testament practice. Methodist preachers were to consider themselves "as *extraordinary messengers,* raised up to provoke the *ordinary* ones to jealousy." They were not appointed to "exercise the priestly office" or to administer the sacraments but to preach and evangelize.[5]

While one might recognize more than two orders of ministry, Wesley thought, still the fundamental distinction was between pastor-priests and preacher-evangelists, the former being "ordinary" ministers and the second "extraordinary." This distinction could be seen even in the Old Testament: "It is true *extraordinary prophets* were frequently raised up, who had not been educated in the 'schools of the prophets', neither had the outward ordinary call. But we read of no *extraordinary priests.*"[6] And in the New Testament and the early church one always finds "if not more, at least two orders distinct from each other, the one having power only to preach and (sometimes) baptize, the other to ordain also and administer the Lord's Supper."[7]

Wesley saw the pastor-priests as the ordinary, established, institutional ministers of the church while the preacher-evangelists were the extraordinary ministers raised up by more immediate divine inspiration somewhat outside institutional channels. Because they were extraordinary, the preacher-evangelists did not share in the more institutional prerogatives of ordaining and administering the sacraments. Thus in the early church, he says,

Both the evangelists and deacons preached. Yea, and women when under extraordinary inspiration. Then both their sons and their daughters prophesied, although in ordinary cases it was not permitted to "a woman to speak in the church." But we do not read in the New Testament that any evangelist or deacon administered the Lord's Supper; much less that any woman administered it, even when speaking by extraordinary inspiration, that inspiration which authorized them for the one not authorizing them for the other. Meanwhile we do read in all the earliest accounts . . . that none but the president or ruling presbyter ever administered the Lord's Supper.[8]

Both orders of ministers were constituted such by the Holy Spirit, however, "for no man or number of men upon earth can constitute an overseer, bishop, or any other Christian minister. To do this is the peculiar work of the Holy Ghost."[9]

Ministry and Gifts Wesley's view of ministry may be described as charismatic since he saw all ministry as springing from the Holy Spirit's work in the church. He used the same ordinary-extraordinary distinction in discussing the gifts of the Spirit that he employed in distinguishing different kinds of ministries, which suggests that he saw ministry and spiritual gifts as being closely related.

While Wesley had no fully developed doctrine of the gifts of the Spirit, he did say enough (mainly in response to charges that he himself pretended to extraordinary gifts or inspirations) to determine his general perspective. His view is complicated by the distinction he made between extraordinary and ordinary gifts, which is not precisely biblical. Among the "extraordinary gifts" he included healing, miracles, prophecy (in the sense of foretelling), discernment of spirits, tongues and the interpretation of tongues, and he describes apostles, prophets and evangelists as "extraordinary officers." The "ordinary gifts" included "convincing speech," persuasion, knowledge, faith, "easy elocution," and pastors and teachers as "ordinary officers."[10] Wesley thus included more than the usually identified *charismata* under "ordinary gifts," and he made a distinction in 1 Corinthians 12 between gifts which were "extraordinary" or "miraculous" and others which were not.[11]

Wesley felt the ordinary gifts were operative in the church in all ages and should appropriately be desired by Christians, though, of course, as secondary to love.[12] All the gifts, including the extraordinary ones, had been part of the experience of the church during the first three centuries, he believed, but "even in the infancy of the church, God divided them with a sparing hand," and principally to those in leadership.[13]

Did Wesley believe the extraordinary gifts could be expected in the church in his day? This, of course, is an important question for the contemporary church. Wesley writes:
It does not appear that these extraordinary gifts of the Holy Ghost were common in the Church for more than two or three centuries. We seldom hear of them after that fatal period when the Emperor Constantine called himself a Christian. . . . From this time they almost totally ceased; very few instances of the kind were found. The cause of this was not, . . . "because there was no more occasion for

them," . . . The real cause was, "the love of many," almost of all Christians, so called, was "waxed cold." . . . This was the real cause why the extraordinary gifts of the Holy Ghost were no longer to be found in the Christian Church.[14]

This did not mean, however, that extraordinary gifts had ceased for all time. God was doing a renewing work through Methodism in his own day, Wesley believed. Thus he nowhere ruled out the possibility of new manifestations of the extraordinary gifts. He felt such gifts either "were designed to remain in the church throughout all ages" or else "they will be restored at the nearer approach of the 'restitution of all things.' "[15] Wesley had a fundamental, although somewhat hidden, optimism regarding such gifts. He advises Christians that the best gifts "are worth your pursuit, though but few of you can attain them."[16] "Perfecting the saints" in Ephesians 4:12 involves "the completing them both in number and their various gifts and graces." Gifts are given for their usefulness, by which "alone are we to estimate all our gifts and talents."[17]

Wesley thus believed that if the extraordinary gifts of the Spirit had practically vanished in his day, this was because of the fallen state of the church and represented a less than ideal situation. In fact God's power was still at work, though hindered by the general coldness and deadness of the church. Wesley certainly did not disparage the gifts, and despite his reticence concerning so-called extraordinary gifts, he valued all gifts and felt that in a truly restored, spiritual church all the gifts would be in evidence.

It was in this context that Wesley understood the gift of tongues. He wrote, "It seems, 'the gift of tongues' was an instantaneous knowledge of a tongue till then unknown, which he that received it could afterwards speak when he thought fit, without any new miracle."[18] He understood tongues as the miraculous ability to speak an actual language, whether previously known or unknown. Because tongues is a gift of language, God might well not give it "where it would be of no use; as in a Church where all are of one mind, and all speak the same language."[19] But if one possesses the gift of tongues he should "not act so absurdly, as to utter in a congregation what can edify none but" himself. Rather he should speak "that tongue, if he find it profitable to himself in his private devotions."[20]

What attitude Wesley would have expressed toward the modern phenomenon of glossolalia remains an open question for several reasons. First, Wesley never had to face precisely this question.[21] Second, Wesley was an experientialist, keenly interested in religious behavior. Considering his reticence either to endorse or condemn rather unusual emotional manifestations in his own meetings, one may conjecture that he would have taken a similarly moderate attitude regarding glossolalia.

Finally, Wesley's strong emphasis on the rational nature of faith does not permit one to say that he would have opposed glossolalia as irrational, for Wesley's view of reason was always tempered by experience. He reacted against an extreme rationalism as much as against any unbiblical "enthusiasm." He was ready to admit that the Christian faith, though rational, also transcends reason. As Albert Outler notes,

Wesley had a remarkably practical rule for judging extraordinary gifts of the Spirit (ecstasies, miracles, etc.). . . . No profession of an "extraordinary gift" ("tongues" or whatever) is to be rejected out of hand, as if we knew what the Spirit should or should not do. He was a cool hand himself, but Wesley had no disdain, on principle, for ecstasies and mind-blowings. What he did insist on was that such gifts are never ends in themselves, that all of them must always be normed (and judged) by the Spirit's "ordinary" gifts ("love, joy, peace, patience, kindness, etc., etc."). Like faith, all spiritual gifts are in order to love, which is the measure of all that is claimed to be from God, since God is love.[22]

While Wesley's view of spiritual gifts is largely undeveloped, he was certainly more aware of, and more positive toward, the *charismata* than most churchmen of his day. Of would-be preachers, he said, it should be asked, "Have they *Gifts* (as well as *Grace)* for the work?"[23] His understanding was complicated, however, by his distinction between ordinary and extraordinary gifts, and for this and other reasons he failed to see the full practical significance of the *charismata* for the "building up" and ministry of the Christian community and to self-consciously connect ministry in the church more closely to the gifts.[24]

If the gifts of the Spirit played a somewhat minor part in Wesley's own theological understanding, however, their exercise played a large part in Methodism. Wesley saw his lay preachers as exercising a charismatic office. They were persons who demonstrated gifts for ministry, and Wesley put them to work, confirming their gifts.

The early Methodist system gave ample room, in fact, for exercising a broad range of spiritual gifts. While such Methodist functions as class leaders, band leaders, assistants, stewards, visitors of the sick, schoolmasters and housekeepers do not seem to have been understood primarily on the basis of the *charismata,* the whole Methodist system in fact encouraged the kind of spiritual growth in which useful charisms would spring forth and be put into redemptive service. Methodism thus provided considerably more opportunity for the exercise of gifts than did the Church of England, where ministry was severely hedged about by clericalism. In this sense Methodist ministry was much more charismatic than were Anglican forms of ministry.

Orders of Ministry   Wesley could accept the traditional threefold distinction of bishops, presbyters (or priests) and deacons, but he saw no essential difference between bishops and presbyters. "By 1755 Wesley was quite convinced," Baker notes, "that in essence there were two orders of minister, with the higher order (which alone was empowered to administer the sacraments and to ordain) subdivided into bishops and presbyters. He completely rejected the notion that there was only one order authorized [both] to preach and to administer" the sacraments.[25] In 1747 Wesley suggested that "the three orders of Bishops, Priests, and Deacons" were plainly evident in the New Testament, but not prescribed for all ages. Rather, there must be "numberless accidental varieties in the government of various churches." "As God variously dispenses His gifts of nature, providence, and grace, both the offices themselves and the officers in each ought to be varied from time to time." Thus Scripture prescribes "no determinate plan of church-government," and there would never have been "any thought of uniformity in the government of all churches" had church leaders "consulted the word of God only."[26] But Wesley still believed "the threefold order of ministers . . . is not only authorized by its apostolical institution, but also by the written Word."[27]

Wesley saw bishops and priests as constituting an "outward priesthood" in the church. "We believe there is, and always was, in every Christian Church (whether dependent on the Bishop of Rome or not), an outward priesthood, ordained by Jesus Christ, and an outward sacrifice offered therein, by men authorized to act as ambassadors of Christ and stewards of the mysteries of God."[28] He viewed this priesthood as a vehicle of sacramental grace, but he rejected the dogma of Trent that ordination itself is a sacrament or that it confers an indelible character.[29] He came to see the priesthood not as primarily mediatorial, but as representative. As Baker notes, *He came to interpret the Lord's Supper as a corporate spiritual action performed by one whom the church had appointed for that purpose. Eventually he used "presbyter" or "elder" in preference to "priest" because of the latter's sacerdotal overtones. Nevertheless, he continued to refer to his own "sacerdotal office," and at the 1755 conference insisted that there was a New Testament priest-*

hood and sacrifice, though this was not a propitiatory sacrifice.[30]

This view of Christian ministry—an "outward priesthood" empowered to ordain and administer the sacraments and an order of "extraordinary ministers" empowered to preach and evangelize—functioned for Wesley in two ways. On the one hand, it was his justification before Anglican critics for appointing Methodist lay preachers. On the other, it was his argument before his preachers for refusing to allow them to give the sacraments or take over other powers of the Anglican clergy. Wesley wanted at all costs to keep this distinction clear and permanent, for it was the key to Methodism's remaining a movement *within* the Church of England rather than becoming a separate sect. As long as Methodist preachers could not give the sacraments, Methodists would have to go to the Anglican service. As long as they could not ordain, there could be no Methodist preachers except those whom Wesley himself appointed. This is precisely what Wesley wanted. In his sermon on "The Ministerial Office" Wesley insisted that he had always appointed Methodist preachers "as Prophets, not as Priests. We received them wholly and solely to preach, not to administer sacraments."[31]

Since Wesley saw no real difference between a bishop and a priest, he felt that biblically he had as much right to ordain as did anyone, although for the sake of order, and to prevent Methodist separation, he was very reluctant to do this. In letters to Charles in later years he said he was convinced he was "a scriptural episkopos as much as any man in England or in Europe,"[32] and that he had as much right to ordain as to administer the Sacrament. "But I see abundance of reasons why I should not use that right, unless I was turned out of the Church."[33]

But Wesley did, in fact, finally ordain ministers for American Methodism. This of course caused sharp controversy and required explanation. As early as 1755 Wesley admitted that in appointing preachers he had already in some sense ordained. Later he justified his ordinations for America on the two grounds of biblical authority and practical necessity. He could earlier have ordained the Methodist preachers in England, but this was unnecessary and would have separated Methodists from the Church of England. "But the case is widely different between England and America," he said. In America there was no one to administer the sacraments to Methodist converts. "Here, therefore, my scruples are at an end; and I conceive myself at full liberty, as I violate no order and invade no man's right by appointing and sending labourers into the harvest."[34]

With this approach Wesley thought he was being at once faithful to Scripture and early church tradition, consistent with a proper understanding of Anglican doctrine, and, above all, obedient to the gospel in seeing to it that the Word was preached as freely and widely as possible. He thought he had found a way to justify both Methodism with its preachers and the institution of the Church of England with its clergy. However we may evaluate Wesley's arguments from our perspective, this was a crucial point for Wesley. It served to mediate between two views of the church and to hold together church and sect without denying the validity of either.

F. Ernest Stoeffler believes Wesley's view of ministry is best explained against the background of Wesley's contacts with Moravianism and the *collegia pietatis* of Continental Pietists. Though Wesley's view might appear ambiguous, Stoeffler argues that the "ambiguities recede into the background if it is remembered that his view of the ministry is related to a conscious adaptation on his part of the *collegia pietatis* arrangement of the church-related Pietists on the Continent, especially as it was observed among the Moravians."[35] I am not convinced that Wesley was consciously imitating or adapting Moravian and Pietist ideas, but he did see Methodism and its ministry as an evangelical order within the Church of England somewhat akin to Pietism within the

Lutheran Church. And he could easily have been influenced by what he saw of Moravian and Pietist models on the Continent.

The Sacraments Wesley's sacramentalism is well known, and he seems most Anglican precisely at this point. But his sacramentalism, like other aspects of his theology and practice, was a modified Anglican position strongly influenced by his evangelical convictions.

Wesley's spiritual renewal in 1738, as Stoeffler notes, influenced his understanding of the sacraments less than it did any other aspect of his theology.[36] But even here one finds a marked shift of emphasis after Aldersgate.

Wesley believed the sacraments were best understood, along with prayer and Bible reading, as means of grace. By "means of grace," Wesley said, "I understand outward signs, words, or actions, ordained of God, and appointed for this end, to be the ordinary channels whereby he might convey to men, preventing, justifying, or sanctifying grace."[37] To call the sacraments "means of grace" suggests both the use and limitations of such ordinances. They must be respected and used, for they convey God's grace. But they are only instruments; they are means, not ends. As the primitive church lost its earlier purity, the means became mistaken for ends. Wesley believed the sacraments, especially the Lord's Supper, were necessary "if not to the *being,* at least to the *well-being* of a Church."[38]

After Aldersgate the ordinances of the church glowed with the living power of the Spirit for Wesley. The interesting thing is that the Lord's Supper took on deeper meaning for Wesley, not less, after his heart-warming experience. Rather than trading off the sacramental means of grace for the direct intimacy of his newfound experience of God, he thrived on them as nourishment for the new life of God in his soul. Here is yet another instance of Wesley's joining the old and new, the institutional and charismatic, and also of keeping the primary accent in its proper place.

Wesley's practice, and to a large degree his theory, of the sacraments varied little from 1725 to the end of his life. But the point of emphasis came increasingly to be on the Spirit of God working *through* the sacraments. Thus he wrote, "All outward means whatever, if separate from the Spirit of God, cannot profit at all, cannot conduce, in any degree, either to the knowledge or love of God. . . . Whosoever, therefore, imagines there is any intrinsic power in any means whatsoever, does greatly err."[39] God is able, said Wesley, to work with or without means. It is the blood of Christ which atones for sin. Yet the means are useful, and "all who desire the grace of God are to wait for it in the means which he hath ordained; in using, not in laying them aside."[40] One should wait for God in the way he has ordained, "expecting that he will meet me there, because he has promised so to do."[41] One should "use all means, *as means;* as ordained, not for their own sake, but in order to the renewal of your soul in righteousness and true holiness. If, therefore, they actually tend to this, well; but if not, they are dung and dross."[42]

For Wesley, the Lord's Supper was a "preventing, justifying, and sanctifying ordinance." That is, it drew a person to God and was instrumental in his justification and sanctification. Thus it was useful and needed at every stage of one's life. The sacraments are for all who are seeking God, not just for the truly converted. The only essential preparation or qualification is a sense of worthlessness, trusting in nothing but God's grace alone. Baker notes that "Wesley never shook off his conviction that for the sake of decency and order, if not for validity and effectiveness, the Lord's Supper must be administered by an ordained clergyman."[43]

The Lord's Supper may properly be called a sacrifice, according to Wesley, but in a very specific sense:

The "unbloody sacrifice" of wine and oil and fine flour was one of the most solemn which was then offered, in the place of which and [of] all the other Jewish sacrifices is the one Christian sacrifice *of bread and wine. This also the ancients termed "the unbloody sacrifice". . . .*

If it be asked, "But is this a propitiatory sacrifice?" I answer, "No." Nor were there ever any such among the Jews. There never was or can be more than one such sacrifice, that offered by "Jesus Christ the righteous."[44]

Wesley's view of baptism was similar but somewhat more ambiguous due to his belief in infant baptism. He felt that in baptism a "principle of grace is infused," and was able to say, "Baptism doth now save us, if we live answerable thereto; if we repent, believe, and obey the gospel: Supposing this, as it admits us into the Church here, so into glory hereafter."[45]

Wesley distinguished between infant baptism and adult baptism, coming close to affirming baptismal regeneration in infants but not in adults. He said of his own experience, "I believe, till I was about ten years old I had not sinned away that 'washing of the Holy Ghost' which was given me in baptism."[46] He held that infants should be baptized because they are guilty of original sin. Baptism washes away original sin, and infants can come to Christ by no other means.[47] He felt that children baptized in infancy were at that time born again and that this was presupposed in the *Book of Common Prayer.* But in the case of adults, at least, a person might be born of water but not yet, or necessarily, of the Spirit.[48] His view is pungently pictured in a 1739 entry in his *Journal:*

I baptized John Smith . . . and four other adults at Islington. Of the adults I have known baptized lately, one only was at that time born again, in the full sense of the word; that is, found a thorough, inward change, by the love of God filling her heart. Most of them were only born again in a lower sense; that is, received the remission of their sins. And some (as it has since too plainly appeared) neither in one sense nor the other.[49]

It will perhaps help in understanding Wesley's view of

baptism to recall his dynamic and experiential conception of conversion and the Christian life. Wesley could say "baptism doth now save us, if we live answereable thereto" because his emphasis was on the present life of God in the soul. Present evidence of the fruit of the Spirit in one's life proved that the new birth had earlier taken place when the believer was baptized. Still, it was not baptism itself, independently, that wrought the change, but the grace of God appropriated by faith.

Summary In his view of the church, its role in history, its structure, ministry and sacraments, Wesley reveals an essentially Anglican position modified and enlivened by his own spiritual rebirth at Aldersgate and by his experiences at the front of a rapidly expanding spiritual movement. The striking thing about Wesley's ecclesiology is that it did not undergo a radical transformation after the critical years of 1738-39. It changed very little. But the changes were of crucial significance, parallel to his personal appropriation of justifying faith through which doctrines mentally accepted became living realities in his own experience.

The changes in Wesley's ecclesiology, as we have seen, were part of a gradual evolution and shift in emphasis which began as early as 1730 and continued through the early years of the revival. Little or no change seems to have occurred in Wesley's view of the church after about 1750. By that time he had arrived securely at the mediating synthesis which was the mark of his ministry and perhaps one of his most significant contributions to the Christian church in all ages.

The meaning of these changes, and the sense in which they make Wesley a radical Christian, are the subject of the final section of this book.

three

WESLEY AND RADICAL
FAITH TODAY

9

WHAT KIND
OF RADICAL?

We hear a lot these days about "radical Christianity" and "radical discipleship." What does it mean? Why the concern?

Renewal in the church has always sparked a new passion to get back to basics—to find the *radix* or root, the peculiar genius of the Christian movement. Times of malaise, anxiety or disillusionment especially sharpen this sense. In the church this concern often becomes "radical" in the secondary, derived sense because of the jarring clash between the unique genius of the church as the community of God's people and the tranquilized, traditionalized, institutionalized and often secularized reality that goes under the name "Christian church."

Crashing into this deep chasm between the church as it is and as it should be according to God's Word easily produces radicals. But that radicality can go in different directions. We see a variety of options demonstrated before us on the current scene. Some folks give up hope and abandon the church altogether. Others give themselves totally to social or political programs in the name of the church but settle for little or no personal involvement with a local Christian community. They may be satisfied with radical action or radical rhetoric without radical community.

There are other options. Some try totally to "start over," junking the institutional church as hopeless, attempting to begin at square one with a new and purer, totally independent form of Christian community. Others, including many in our own day, form new intentional communities of various kinds which attempt faithfulness to radical gospel demands but also continuity with the larger church and some cooperation with existing church structures.[1] Another seemingly growing group is rediscovering the mystery and majesty of the historic Christian tradition and channeling the concern for radicality into a new awareness of the meaning of sacrament.[2]

Where does John Wesley fit into this strange scene? What was the nature of *his* radicality? And what might his thought and example teach us today?

In this final section of the book I wish to examine Wesley in the light of these concerns. We will look at three questions. First, what kind of Christian radicality does Wesley really represent? And, so what?

Second, what does Wesley's experience and that of early Methodism suggest about the way renewal occurs in the church? Does this example of renewal fit any kind of recognizable pattern of continuing relevance?

Finally, what specific, practical lessons can we learn from Wesley for the life and structure of the Christian community?

Thus we will look at the nature of Wesley's radicality, the larger question of renewal movements and the more particular concern of Christian congregational life.

Wesley as Radical Wesley's understanding of the church and Christian discipleship might be defined in different ways. As noted previously, Wesley has been explained in terms of Anglo-Catholic, Puritan-Reformed, Lutheran and to a lesser extent specifically free church traditions. All of these discussions yield helpful insights.

For several reasons it seems useful here to look at Wesley

especially in the light of the Anabaptist or Radical Protestant tradition. Wesley has seldom been examined from this perspective, and yet, as noted above, Anabaptism today is providing one of the primary paradigms for radical Christians and Christian communities. It is a tradition in which the question of the life and style of the church is a central issue. Here is a tradition that answers the question "What kind of radicality?" by saying that the church must be a distinct, separate, countercultural covenant community if it is to speak prophetically to the world and the institutional church. For these reasons it provides a useful background for understanding Wesley's particular brand of radical Christianity.

Is Wesley also among the Radical Protestants? How could he possibly be when he lived and died a High Church Anglican, a loyal son of an established, institutional church?

The crucial events in Wesley's life from 1738 to 1740 pushed him in directions parallel to Radical Protestantism. Over a span of a dozen or so years after Aldersgate Wesley came to the particular understanding of the church which we have outlined. Many of Wesley's contemporaries saw him as an "enthusiast," a fanatic, a radical. He was the center of anti-Methodist pamphlets and tracts accusing him of being everything from a papist to a heretic. But how similar in his theory and practice of the church was Wesley to the Radical Protestants?

We first need a working definition of Radical Protestantism based in the actual history of the church. It won't do simply to take the Moravians, Anabaptists or some other similar group as the measure of Radical Protestantism. On the other hand, several of these groups show significant points of similarity. Examining these similarities yields a working model or typology of Radical Protestantism.

From some perspectives John Wesley and early Methodism were not unique in history. Striking similarities between Methodism and the Waldenses of twelfth-century France, for instance, can be documented—such as primitivism, itinerant preaching, an emphasis on the gospel for the poor and "faith working by love."[3] Several writers have noted Wesleyan parallels with Francis of Assisi or even Ignatius Loyola, classmate of John Calvin and founder of the Jesuits.[4] Ronald Knox noted, "Wesley's open-air sermons, lay preachers, and institution of a church within the church have so often been compared to the Mendicant revival of the twelfth century that we might expect to find in Wesley an admirer of St. Francis."[5] But in fact Wesley apparently said nothing about Francis. In his own day Wesley's critics routinely condemned him by showing the ways he was like the Franciscans or Jesuits.

Francis, Waldo and Wesley and the renewal movements springing from them (the Franciscans, Waldenses and Methodists) could be compared as differing models of renewal within the larger context of the church. Other possible parallels might include modern Pentecostalism and particularly the Catholic charismatic renewal, which, like Wesleyanism, stresses the experiential side of the faith and faces similar difficulties to those of Wesleyanism in seeking to be a self-conscious subcommunity or *ecclesiola* working to revitalize and yet remain loyal to the larger church body.[6]

All these renewing forces were in one way or another radical departures from the status quo. We will particularly examine the Radical Protestant tradition as embodied in the believers' churches and especially in sixteenth-century Anabaptism because from one perspective Methodism is closely akin to this tradition. Here the Moravian Brethren are important in their direct link with Wesley as mediators of Radical Protestantism.

The Radical Protestant Model   Radical Protestantism finds its fundamental paradigms in sixteenth-century Anabaptism and later movements closely connected with it. For purposes of comparison we may build a Radical Protestant model. This involves extracting, somewhat artificially, the essential or most characteristic features found in differing periods and contexts. If defined too broadly, such a model becomes so vague as to be unhelpful, while if too narrowly it fails to distinguish adequately between a pure type and the particular historical circumstances. The following model is constructed from descriptions given by several contemporary scholars—particularly Donald Durnbaugh, Franklin Littell, William Estep and John Howard Yoder.[7]

Four succinct statements suggest the basic ingredients of Radical Protestantism as it has appeared historically. George H. Williams speaks of "the gathered church of committed believers living in the fellowship of mutual correction, support, and abiding love."[8] Donald Durnbaugh says the church is "the covenanted and disciplined community of those walking in the way of Jesus Christ."[9] Speaking specifically of Anabaptism, Harold S. Bender sees discipleship as "the most characteristic, most central, most essential and regulative concept in Anabaptist thought, which largely determines all else."[10] Similarly, Franklin Littell says that "the essence of Anabaptist concern was the nature of discipleship, conceived in terms of Christian community; in short, the view of the Church."[11]

In other words, Radical Protestants are concerned with both belief and life. And often the primary accent falls on life—the *way* of following Jesus Christ—based on the sure conviction that life is the only true measure of real faith. So Radical Protestantism is Christian discipleship—not in isolation but in community. It is the "joyful community" of those who have traded everything else for the privilege of banding together around the person and example of Jesus Christ and the cause of his Kingdom.

The Radical Protestant model may be said to consist of the following seven elements:

1. Voluntary adult membership based on a covenant-commitment to Jesus Christ, emphasizing obedience to Jesus as necessary evidence of faith in him. Believers' baptism has usually been the sign of this commitment, but not always. The point is not, fundamentally, the *form* of joining the covenant community but the *fact* and *meaning* of conscious committed membership in it.

2. A community or brotherhood of discipline, edification, correction and mutual aid, in conscious separation from the world, as the primary visible expression of the church.

3. A life of good works, service and witness as an expression of Christian love and obedience expected of all believers. Thus there is an emphasis on the ministry of the laity, rather than of a special ministerial class and the church is viewed as "a missionary minority."

4. The Spirit and the Word as comprising the sole basis of authority, implying a de-emphasis on or rejection of church traditions and creeds.

5. Primitivism and restitutionism. The early church is the model, and the goal is to restore the essential elements of early church life and practice. This usually implies some view of the fall of the church as well.

6. A pragmatic, functional approach to church order and structure.

7. A belief in the universal church as the body of Christ, of which the particular visible believing community is but a part.

These seven items provide a comprehensive model of the Radical Protestant understanding of the church. Other themes might be mentioned, such as suffering, the eschatological vision, pacifism, consensus in decision making, ecumenism and separation from the state. These have been important themes among some, but not all, Radical Protestants. But the seven elements listed here are basic and not so closely dependent on particular historical circumstances.

They are also those most often cited by students of the Radical Protestant tradition.

Wesley and Radical Protestantism   Does Wesley fit the Radical Protestant model, either in theory or in practice?

Franklin Littell says of Wesley,

Throughout his active life he shifted by steady steps from the developmental and sacramental view of the institutions of Christendom to normative use of the New Testament and reference to the Early Church. He justified field preaching and the itineracy, class meetings and their disciplinary structure, and finally the ordination of ministers for America, on the argument that he was following "apostolic" practice. He became, in his basic orientation, a Free Churchman.[12]

True—but without ever rejecting Anglicanism or a sacramental view of the church. It is helpful therefore to examine the seven elements of the Radical Protestant model in the light of Wesley's life and theology.

1. *Voluntary adult membership based on a covenant-commitment to Jesus Christ, emphasizing obedience to Jesus as a necessary evidence of faith in him.*

Adult baptism and a rejection of infant baptism have often been considered *the* distinguishing marks of Radical Protestantism. But the more basic issue, as several scholars have noted, is voluntarism: the church as a covenant community of freely acting adults. Believers' baptism has usually been the sign, since the person baptized in infancy makes no decision about becoming part of the church. But the more basic question is voluntary commitment, for even the infant-baptized adult can make an adult covenant commitment, even if this is not called baptism.

Wesley of course insisted on infant baptism, although his views on baptism were somewhat ambiguous. He clearly saw the need for conscious adult commitment and obedience to the gospel. He strongly stressed a conscious, rational decision to accept and follow Jesus. This was, in fact, the whole point of having "a people called Methodists." To be a member of a Methodist society meant that one had submitted to accepted rules and disciplines. Wesley used an annual covenant service as one means for reinforcing and renewing the personal commitment of each believer.

An ambiguity arises here, however, one that applies to all the elements of the Radical Protestant model. Wesley insisted on voluntary adult commitment as a condition *for becoming a Methodist*. But the peculiar place of Methodism within the Church of England, and Wesley's Anglican ecclesiology, must be remembered. Wesley could assume that his Methodists had already been baptized as infants in the Church of England. Voluntary adult commitment was necessary therefore to become a Methodist, but not to be part of the Church of England. Which, however, was more truly the church? Wesley believed the Church of England was a true church but seriously degenerate, while Methodism showed what the whole church *should* be like.

Had Wesley concluded that the Church of England was totally apostate, things would of course have been different. He might then well have decided that infant baptism in the state church was meaningless, if not detrimental, and therefore have begun baptizing his Methodist converts. He thus would have in fact become an "anabaptist," a rebaptizer. But, due to his continued, if qualified, acceptance of the validity and normative role of the institutional church, Wesley never fully adopted an Anabaptist position.

Yet within the societies, while continuing to accept many High Church views and to contend for infant baptism, Wesley did stress voluntary adult membership. And one gets the impression from reading Wesley that he felt his Methodist societies were more genuinely the church than was the Church of England, though Wesley would hardly have said as much.

From a logical standpoint, one might suppose that if Wesley wanted to see Anglicanism become more like Methodism, he would have called for membership being restricted to adult commitment and would therefore have opposed infant baptism. Wesley, however, was deeply committed to the sacramental mystery of the church, and his own spiritual life was constantly nourished by frequent celebration of the Lord's Supper. Thus he always felt that infant baptism was in some way efficacious and never thoroughly addressed this paradox in his own convictions.

2. *A community or brotherhood of discipline, edification, correction and mutual aid, in conscious separation from the world, as the primary visible expression of the church.*

Wesley clearly parallels the Radical Protestant model at this point. His use of bands, classes and societies confirms this, as do his writings. Wesley saw himself as imitating the primitive church in bringing Methodists together in close-knit societies. The classes and bands provided discipline, correction and mutual aid on the New Testament pattern. Since the class meeting became the gate to the Methodist society and the mechanism for excluding unruly members, it tended to make Methodism as distinct, disciplined and consistent a group of believers as were the earlier Anabaptists.

Wesley, as deeply conscious of the communal nature of the church as were the Anabaptists, insisted that "Christianity is essentially a social religion" rather than a "solitary religion"; "I mean not only that it cannot subsist so well, but that it cannot subsist at all, without society—without living and conversing with other men."[13] Wesley developed this theme, however, in a somewhat different and politically less radical way than did the Anabaptists. The reasons for this lie in the historical circumstances. While the Methodist societies, classes and bands formed a distinct subcommunity within the Church of England, they were never forced by the civil and religious power structure to become a separate and distinct sect. This accounts for much of the difference between early Methodism and such groups as the Mennonites and Hutterites.

Franklin Littell compares Wesley with Menno Simons, founder of the Mennonites, and finds striking similarities at the point of discipline and discipleship. Both Menno and Wesley "dealt with Christian perfection in terms of the New Testament imperatives, in terms of the perfection of the church," introducing a "radical discontinuity between the 'world' . . . and the disciplines of discipleship."[14] Both spoke of the "circumcision of the heart." Littell notes that with both men "the entire problematic is set in the context of the church, with Christian perfection a matter of community witness and not individual enterprise." Both Menno and Wesley stressed positive discipline and introduced means for exercising such discipline.[15] In this connection it is interesting that Menno was converted to Anabaptism directly from Roman Catholicism without passing through Reformation Protestantism. Like Wesley, he combined Catholic and evangelical strains.

Wesley's concept of Christian perfection was, of course, somewhat different from Menno's.[16] The point here, however, is the similarity at the point of the ecclesiological meaning of the perfection emphasis. When we see how Wesley's stress on sanctification actually worked itself out in the system of societies, classes and bands, we are struck with the degree to which Christian perfection for Wesley actually meant discipleship, not just an interior work of grace in the believer. In later Wesleyan interpretation this link between sanctification and discipleship (and its enabling structures) was, unfortunately, largely severed. Colin Williams is right in observing:

Wesley believed that the necessity for mutual encouragement, mutual examination, and mutual service, within the context of the means of grace, required more than the hearing of the Word, the partici-

pation in the sacraments, and the joining in the prayers of the "great congregation." Wesley's view of holiness was woven into his ecclesiology. *He believed that the gathering together of believers into small voluntary societies for mutual discipline and Christian growth was essential to the Church's life.*[17]

On this point Wesley's church concept clearly fits the Radical Protestant mold.

3. *A life of good works, service and witness as an expression of Christian love and obedience expected of all believers.*

Wesley's stress on good works was characteristic of his Anglican theology. He was confident believers could, by God's grace, work effectively to improve both themselves and their world. The Christian, born again by grace, was called to "all inward and outward holiness," to do all the good possible.

Wesley did not, however, work out a coherent doctrine of lay ministry or the priesthood of believers. His rather elaborate view of ministry was intended to justify both Anglican structure and his use of lay preachers. Thus his argument tended to spring from his Anglican commitments rather than from a conviction that all believers are called to minister on the basis of the *charismata* or the spiritual priesthood. Wesley's practice went further than his theory, however, for Methodism was largely a lay movement, involving thousands of unordained folks in a wide range of leadership and ministry functions.

Wesley especially insisted that faith did not excuse one from a life of good works, just as he insisted there could be no good works without faith. Love is the fulfilling of the law, "not by releasing us from, but by constraining us to obey it."[18] Thus Wesley said,

(1) Whether they will finally be lost or saved, you are expressly commanded to feed the hungry, and clothe the naked. If you can, and do not, whatever becomes of them, you shall go away into everlasting fire. (2) Though it is God only changes hearts, yet he generally doeth it by man. It is our part to do all that in us lies, as diligently as if we

could change them ourselves, and then to leave the event to him. (3) God, in answer to their prayers, builds up his children by each other in every good gift; nourishing and strengthening the whole "body by that which every joint supplieth."[19]

For Wesley, holiness and good works were all of one piece. He saw "faith, holiness and good works as the root, the tree, and the fruit, which God had joined and man ought not to put asunder."[20] He especially stressed prayer, the Eucharist, Bible study, feeding the hungry, clothing the naked, helping the stranger, and visiting or relieving the sick and imprisoned.[21] He would have disputed any claim to holiness not marked by good works. Thus at this point, too, Wesley evidences strong affinities with the Radical Protestant model.

4. *The Spirit and the Word as comprising the sole basis of authority, implying a de-emphasis on or rejection of church tradition and creeds.*

On this point Wesley shifted decidedly toward the Radical Protestant perspective. As noted earlier, he was firmly committed to the "Anglican triad" of Scripture, reason and antiquity as the basis of authority—or, more accurately, the "Wesleyan quadrilateral" of Scripture, reason, tradition and experience. Reason remained strong in Wesley's system; he constantly appealed to "men of reason and religion." With time, however, three things happened in Wesley's use of this basis of authority: First, "antiquity" came increasingly to mean the precedents of early Christianity, rather than later church tradition. Second, reason came to mean that which could be seen as reasonable in the light of experience. Wesley appealed to reason not as an abstract principle, but as a pragmatic test and, as George Croft Cell showed at length, experience itself became an important basis of authority and insight.[22] Third, Wesley came to view Scripture and tradition less in terms of the letter and more in terms of the spirit, particularly the animating Holy Spirit.

Wesley began to study the Bible seriously in 1729, convinced that it was "the only standard of truth, and the only model of pure religion."[23] "I allow no other rule," he wrote in 1739, "whether of faith or practice, than the Holy Scriptures."[24] Salvation was accomplished as the Spirit applied the Word in the heart: "all true faith, and the whole work of salvation, every good thought, word, and work, is altogether by the operation of the Spirit of God."[25] It was by this dynamic view of the Spirit that Wesley's "evangelical synergism" was guarded from Pelagianism or works righteousness. Characteristically, however, Wesley's stress on the Spirit and the Word did not mean a rejection of the creeds or church tradition. These were placed in a decidedly secondary position, but Wesley insisted on their proper role in that position.

5. *Primitivism and restitutionism.*

Wesley's concern with early church life and practice reflected current tendencies in some branches of Anglicanism. But Wesley's was a practical concern, not just an intellectual one. The primitivist motif marked Wesley's thinking and practice from 1729 on. The chief change in Wesley's thinking on this point was the stress upon the spirit rather than the letter. Still, he was pleased whenever he could point to a parallel between some specific innovation and early church practice.

At this point also Wesley fits the Radical Protestant mold. Although other Anglican divines shared some of his primitivism, Wesley's desire to recapture the dynamic of the early church was a practical motivating force pushing him toward innovation and helping to justify new methods.

6. *A pragmatic, functional approach to church order and structure.*

Wesley shared this trait with Radical Protestant leaders and movements. He was able to satisfy himself that his innovations were justified either as having early church precedent or as being born of necessity, or both. His pragmatism was, he felt, therefore both reasonable and scriptural.

Wesley's pragmatism was theologically based, as it was with earlier Radical Reformers. Church structure was a secondary question, Wesley felt. No specific form was essential to the church nor prescribed in Scripture. This is one point at which Wesley's views changed considerably from 1729 to 1745, as already noted. It was also a major point of controversy, for relatively few Anglican leaders were ready to follow Wesley in his structural innovations. It was one thing to admit that Anglican structures were pragmatically justified; it was quite another to suggest on pragmatic grounds that they ought to be changed!

Wesley's whole career shows that his pragmatism in no way indicated indifference or insensitivity to church structure. On the contrary, Wesley felt keenly the importance of form and structure. As early as his Oxford days he took special interest in such questions. He came to see, however, that such matters could best be settled on pragmatic, functional grounds, for very little structure was prescribed in Scripture, hoary church tradition notwithstanding. This gave him a freedom to move and to use his own organizing genius in ways that reinforced and nourished the life of Christian experience and community which very clearly *was* revealed in the Bible. It was Wesley's freedom from forms many thought were sacred that in fact freed him to be biblical at a more fundamental level.

For all his pragmatism, however, Wesley remained a conservative at heart. His principles were plain: change nothing that does not need changing; but change anything that clogs the free flow of the gospel. Evident here is the same mixture of conservatism and pragmatism that marked all Wesley's life and thought.

7. *A belief in the universal church as the body of Christ, of which the particular visible believing community is but a part.*

Some may question whether this element should be included in a Radical Protestant model since practically all

Christians share some form of belief in the church universal. Historically, however, this has been an especially strong motif in the Radical Protestant tradition. The Radical Reformers argued that the church was visible not in its hierarchy or structure but in its concrete existence as a believing community.

So it was with Wesley. He believed in the universal church and saw it consisting especially in the whole body of Christian believers.

Summary Using Radical Protestantism as a model, we emerge with a clearer sense of Wesley's own brand of radical Christian faith. At practically every point Wesley incorporated the emphases and concerns of the Radical Protestant tradition. But he did so as an established churchman. He did so as one who refused to surrender "both-and" for the seeming inevitability of "either-or."

Partly because of this, representatives of different traditions have made different claims on Wesley as one of their own. This is understandable precisely because of the mixture in Wesley of old and new, tradition and innovation, the institutional and the charismatic. Colin Williams suggests,

Do we not see . . . in Wesley a creative attempt to keep all three historic emphases together? . . . The Catholic emphasis is right–Christ does not abandon his Church, even when the priests are unfaithful, but is always present in unbroken continuity in the sacraments he has provided. The Classical Protestant emphasis is right–the pure witness to the faith once delivered to the saints is essential to the ever renewed "event" in which believers are called into being. . . . The Free Church emphasis is right–true believers must be gathered together for mutual growth in the life of the Spirit toward the fullness of the stature of Christ.[26]

This is a fair assessment, though one might not wish to express these three emphases precisely in these terms. And yet just for these reasons Wesley is a radical Christian. Christian radicality does not reject either the evangelical or the Catholic emphasis but insists that at all costs the church must be a visible community that takes seriously the demands of discipleship.

10
PATTERNS
OF RENEWAL

Methodism under John Wesley became a massive movement of the common people, the "disinherited masses" to whom the gospel was totally foreign. It grew into a disciplined movement which made some people nervous—church leaders, because the authority of the established church seemed threatened; political authorities, because they feared what would happen if Methodism became a political crusade. The fears are understandable, for in the late 1700s Methodists were quite simply the most disciplined, cohesive and self-conscious large body of people in England.

But Methodism was, above all, a movement of spiritual renewal. It was a mass movement of people coming to know the power of God and the power of genuine Christian community in their daily lives. It is therefore one of the primary examples in history of the renewing work of the Holy Spirit.

The causes of any great spiritual awakening are doubtless complex and not fully open to investigation. Still, study of Scripture and God's work in history does reveal some of the elements in renewal. Richard F. Lovelace has done a very creditable job of analyzing many such factors in his recent book, *Dynamics of Spiritual Life: An Evangelical Theology of Renewal.*[1] Lovelace sees patterns of cyclical renewal fitting into a more basic oscillating pattern of continuous renewal. He traces what he sees as the preconditions and the primary and secondary elements in spiritual renewal, and then draws a basic picture of the church's missionary movement as "an army of liberation progressively freeing and clearing territory from demonic control in a pulsating series of advances and temporary fallbacks." Lovelace suggests that "the church will continue to experience massive general awakenings right up to the end of its career in history, when Christ will return to deliver it from the last and greatest counterattack of the powers of darkness."[2]

Without going into a discussion of all the elements Lovelace suggests as factors in renewal, one can at least affirm that successive renewal movements often do follow discernible patterns. Thus parallels between various movements in time can be traced. Methodism under John Wesley had much in common with other movements of renewal, despite its unique features. In the present chapter I wish to outline a pattern of spiritual renewal which, it seems to me, is a fundamental component of the larger picture of the Spirit's renewing and liberating work in the church and in the world.

Wesley's View of Methodism Lovelace stresses Christian fellowship or community as one of the essential elements in renewal. He sees the Moravian community at Herrnhut as "the most thoroughgoing and fruitful application of the principle of community in church history" and believes Moravianism "suggests a paradigm for the transformation of the whole church."[3] Moravianism was to be a renewing cell within the church, drawing its strength from intimate community.

As we have noted, Wesley was indebted to the Moravians for some features of early Methodist structure, most notably, the bands. He was deeply conscious that Methodism constituted a distinct community, "the people called Methodists." He pondered the meaning of Methodism as a movement and noted with great interest the depth and intimacy of community that developed in the Methodist societies, classes and bands.

To Wesley, Methodism was not just an English version of Moravianism but was a "new thing" brought forth by God—unique because it centered in Christian life and experience, not a creed, and because it remained a reforming body *within* the church, rather than separating from it. In 1755 he wrote, "We look upon the *Methodists* in general, not as any particular party (this would exceedingly obstruct the Grand Design for which we conceive God has raised them up) but as living witnesses in and to every part of that Christianity which we preach, which is hereby demonstrated to be a real thing, and visibly held out to all the world."[4] He argued that the Methodists' "peculiar glory" was that they did not split off to become a distinct sect or erect barriers of creed and practice. Methodists "do not separate from the religious community to which they at first belonged; they are still members of the Church."[5] He told his followers, "Ye are a new phenomenon in the earth,—a body of people who, being of no sect or party, are friends to all parties, and endeavour to forward all in heart-religion, in the knowledge and love of God and man."[6] Wesley wrote such things, of course, partly to counteract the drift toward separation from the Church of England that he perceived emerging within Methodism.

Wesley especially stressed that joining the Methodists was not a matter of creed or liturgical practice. He observed,

In order to their union with us, we require no unity in opinions, or in modes of worship, but barely that they "fear God and work righteousness," . . . Now, this is utterly a new thing, unheard of in any other Christian community. In what Church or congregation beside, throughout the Christian world, can members be admitted upon these terms, without any other conditions? . . . This is the glory of the Methodists, and of them alone! They are themselves no particular sect or party; but they receive those, of all parties, who "en-

deavour to do justly, and love mercy, and walk humbly with their God."[7]

This did not mean, of course, that Wesley or the Methodists were indifferent to matters of doctrine or liturgy. Wesley assumed the basic creedal and liturgical framework of the Church of England and saw Methodism as a renewing movement within the larger church (though one did not have to be an Anglican to be a Methodist).

When Wesley said the Methodists were "no particular party or sect," he was certainly not denying, however, the corporate nature and identity of the Methodists. They were *"a people* called Methodists"; they were a "society," a distinct community within the Church; an *ecclesiola;* an evangelical order. Wesley understood Methodism's place as natural and healthy, if unique, within the Church of England. The Methodists did not want to be a separate sect living only for themselves. They existed for the health and renewal of the whole body. Wesley regarded Methodism as a movement of authentic Christianity *within* the larger church, which was largely decadent.

Durward Hofler notes that while Wesley claimed the Methodist societies were merely Christian subcommunities within the larger church, yet he defined "church" in terms that in fact were descriptive of Methodism. Wesley regarded the Methodist societies "as groups within, supplemental, and subordinate to the Church of England. Yet according to his own definition of a church as a group of believers, the Methodist societies were at least spiritual churches within the Anglican Church. . . . His very actions showed that he in fact regarded the societies as churches."[8]

All of this suggests that Wesley viewed the Methodist societies as *ecclesiolae* or "little churches" within the *ecclesia,* the church. Although Wesley does not seem to have used the term, Methodism was in fact an *ecclesiola,* both in theory and practice. George H. Williams suggests that Wesley till his death thought of the Methodist societies "as primarily the Evangelical *ecclesiolae* within the rationalist, moralistic Established Church of England."[9] Similarly, Albert Outler comments that "Wesley's idea of the Methodist societies serving the Established Church even against the good will of her leaders was a distinctive adaptation of the pietistic pattern of the 'religious societies' *(ecclesiolae in ecclesiam)* which Anthony Horneck had brought from Germany to England in 1661 and which had served as a refuge for 'serious Christians,' discontent with apathetic and nominal Christianity."[10]

But if Methodism was "a church within the church"— *ecclesiola in ecclesia*—what, in fact, was the larger church, the *ecclesia*? The obvious answer is the Church of England. But for Wesley the universal church, even in England, was broader than the Anglican communion. Wesley's willingness to allow non-Anglican Dissenters into the Methodist societies and his openness to the Moravians and other groups show that he saw Methodism as an evangelical order, not within the Church of England only, but within the universal church. The *ecclesia* was not just Anglicanism; it was broader. And Methodism was out to reform not just the Church of England, but the Christian church everywhere.

Thus Wesley's view of the church and of the role of Methodism transcended the idea merely of a reforming party within a particular established church communion. Like many radical Christians before and after, Wesley had a dual focus: The authentic life and witness of the visible local community of believers, and the universal body of Christ spread throughout the world without which the local congregation was incomplete.

Perhaps Wesley's understanding and the experience of Methodism provide the raw materials for understanding one way renewal comes to the church.

Toward a Model of Renewal   Typically questions of church renewal have been viewed in one of two ways. They have been seen either from what may be called the institutional or the charismatic perspective (understanding neither term pejoratively). This distinction is roughly parallel to Ernst Troeltsch's distinction between church and sect.

The Institutional View. From this perspective, the church is God's saving institution on earth. Church history is seen positively as the unfolding drama of God's purposes. The given structures of the church (theological and especially organizational) are not fundamentally questioned. Periods of decline or unfaithfulness in church history stem from the personal character of church leaders or external factors, but not from the church-as-institution itself. In fact, the institutional stability and survival of the church in spite of periods of decline, opposition or weakness are seen as part of the glory of the church. They reveal God's providence in establishing the church as the institution of salvation.

Thus from a Roman Catholic perspective the survival of the papacy in spite of periods of corruption or weakness attests to the validity of the church. Or similarly, from a Protestant perspective, the endurance of preaching or the "ministerial office" is seen as a source of God's renewing work even when many people are unfaithful.

From this perspective, nothing is ever fundamentally wrong with the church. The question of church renewal, therefore, is exclusively (or nearly so) a question of the spiritual renewal of individual persons or the general body of believers. Thus one of Philip Spener's opponents could argue, "It is not the Church but the ungodly in the Church that must be reformed."[11] The problem is simply that people fail to believe or act as the church tells them to. Renewal, however it comes, means restoring people to the level of belief or action defined by the church as normal. And any genuine renewal is seen as beginning with the ecclesiastical leaders and affecting the whole church more or less evenly.

From the institutional perspective, any kind of renewal movement immediately provokes suspicion, if not actual hostility. A new structure dedicated to church renewal is intuitively, and correctly, perceived by the keepers of the institution as calling into question (at least potentially) the validity of the institutional church itself, at least in its given form. Thus tension is inevitable, and the results are predictable. The renewal body will either: (1) become increasingly radicalized and eventually leave or be forced out of the institutional church, as with the Waldenses and the Methodists (and inevitably, it seems, forces are at work on both sides tending toward schism or separation); (2) lose its vitality to the point where it is no longer a threat to the institutional church (the Continental Pietists); or (3) become accommodated to the institutional church by being given a recognized but limited place within the structure (as with Catholic religious orders). All three of these options seem to be compatible with a greater or lesser degree of renewing impact on the church by the renewal structure or movement.

The Charismatic View. In the charismatic view, the church in any age must be in direct contact with God and a clear channel of his grace *(charis)* in order to have life and power. The church is essentially a spiritual organism and community, whatever its institutional form may be. Institutional forms are viewed ambivalently or totally rejected.

The charismatic view naturally sees church history in a different light. History and tradition do not automatically validate the present form of the church. Since the stress is on immediate and direct spiritual life, history is evaluated according to evidence of such life at various points in the past and according to whether past events are seen as contributing to or undermining the church's spiritual life.

The charismatic view is especially attracted to the picture of the primitive church in the New Testament, or to an idealized model of that picture, and typically measures the history and present state of the church by this picture (primitivism). Since any substantial decline from the New Testament ideal must be explained without calling God's existence, sovereignty or immediate availability into question, this line of reasoning leads naturally to some theory of the fall of the church and to the present need to restore the church to its primitive purity (restitutionism).

Because of its emphasis on immediate experience and its religious idealism, the charismatic view is typically concerned with the whole experience of the church and with the visible expression of the church as a renewed community and people, not just with private, individual experience. This places it in conflict with the institutional view, because champions of the charismatic view typically perceive (often correctly) that many of the obstacles to renewal are enshrined in traditional and institutional forms. Either these forms must change, or, failing that, a more renewed and virile form of Christian community must be implanted within the institutional church so that the charismatic ideal may become a reality (*ecclesiola;* the Pietist *collegium pietatis;* the Moravian communities and bands; the Methodist societies and classes).

Thus the same three options emerge. Depending partly on the radicality of the charismatic group and its critique of the institutional church, and partly on the response or reaction from the institutional church, the renewal group will either: (1) form a totally separate body or sect; (2) dry up and blow away; or (3) strike a deal with the institutional church which allows it some autonomy in exchange for its recognition of the authority and validity of the institutional "powers that be." Again, which of these options occurs depends not just on the spiritual temperature of the renewing body but also on other factors, and on the response or reaction of the institutional church to the would-be renewers.

A Mediating Perspective. Is there any middle ground here? Can both views be incorporated into one understanding of the church and church renewal which affirms both the necessity of a present, vital experience of Christian community and discipleship and also the validity of the church in its more institutional form?

In the first place, both the institutional and charismatic views are open to criticism. The institutional view is often blind to the great gulf between the church's profession and its possession, and to its own institutionalism and self-interest in keeping its status at approximately quo. Consequently it often underrates the truth in the charismatic claim and misreads the importance of the renewal movement. Thus it finds itself in the unfortunate position of fighting in practice the very things it favors in theory.

But the charismatic view has similar problems. The renewers often have no sense of history (or force history into an ideological framework) and too easily identify God's purposes exclusively with their side in the renewal debate. They are typically naive concerning institutional and sociological realities and blind to the institutional dimensions of their own movement. In their concern with present experience they may fall prey to bizarre apocalyptic, dispensational or millennial views which are unbiblical and unrealistic and may lead to extreme hopes, claims or behavior.

On the other hand, both views have their strengths. Whatever the church's state of decline, it still carries (except in the most extreme cases) the Scriptures, the sacraments and a deposit of Christian doctrinal truth. The very birth of a renewal body is presumptive evidence that some spiritual life still remains in the old church. And if one takes historical processes seriously, some real continuity—and therefore validity—must be granted to the institutional church. Otherwise the renewal movement would have to be seen as a *totally* new, unique and unprecedented phenomenon, a church *sui generis* or one generated uniquely by the Spirit's action unrelated to history. Such a view would be unbiblical as well as sociologically and historically naive.

Similarly, the charismatic view cannot be totally rejected on either biblical or sociological grounds. Institutions decline and need periodic renewal. When the institution is the church, the renewal certainly must spring from or result in a new or renewed *experience* of God's grace, whatever other features it may have. Further, the charismatic stress on community and on charismatic (rather than institutional, authoritarian) leadership often points to real problem areas in the institutional church. And one cannot deny the internal dynamism of many renewal movements nor that, in many cases, this dynamism has contributed largely to the renewal or rebirth of the institutional church itself (for example, the Franciscan movement). This dynamism must be accounted for in some way. If evaluated spiritually, it presumably is either good or bad. If the renewal is in fact biblically based, shows the marks of the New Testament church and sparks new life throughout the church, it can only be evaluated favorably, whatever its weaknesses. And even if evaluated on purely sociological grounds, the beneficial impact of the renewing force on the institutional church would presumably have to be admitted.

If this line of reasoning is correct, it logically points toward a theory of church life and renewal which *combines* insights from the institutional and charismatic views. This would point toward a mediating model of the church which seeks not merely to steer a middle course between the two views but to incorporate the truth of both.

Such a mediating model would need, then, to see both the institutional church (even when in periods of decline) and also renewal movements and forces as in some sense valid and perhaps even normal. Obviously not all renewal movements are equally beneficial. From a Christian theological standpoint the validity of particular renewal movements would have to be settled on primarily biblical grounds. But a mediating model would expect renewal movements to arise and would anticipate their making a genuine biblical and spiritual contribution to the life of the church.

Analogies may be useful in exploring such a mediating model. Most biblical figures of the church are figures from life—body, tree, vine, marriage and so forth. We may notice a figure found in Isaiah 11:1 and elsewhere, the figure of an old, partially deadened growth sending forth new shoots. Renewal movements seem almost instinctively drawn toward such analogies. The movement represents "new life," a sprouting forth of new growth. But the analogy necessarily implies that some life still remains in the old stock, that both have sprung from the same roots. In short, this is a mediating figure.

The stock-and-branch metaphor suggests an interdependence or symbiosis between the institutional church and the renewal movement. It recognizes that, for whatever reason, the stock has lost an earlier vigor, but that it still has life and, therefore, hope. And it recognizes that the new branch has not sprung into being simply on its own but to some degree has its source (whatever other influences may be at work) in the old stock.

Roman Catholic theologian Rosemary Ruether, author of *The Radical Kingdom*, suggests essentially this model in her essay, "The Free Church Movement in Contemporary Catholicism."[12] Ruether describes the free church and the institutional church as "interdependent polarities" in the normal life of the church. She writes:

The free church, in the sense I am using it, is the free community within historical Christianity. It is founded on a view of the church which denies that hierarchical institutionalization belongs to the essence of the church. The church is seen essentially as the gathered community of explicit believers in which sacramental distinctions between clergy and laity are abolished, priestly roles become purely contextual and functional; the whole community arising by joint covenant entered into by the existential analogue of believer's baptism; that is to say, by voluntary adult decision. This concept of the believer's church is, I believe, the authentic church, and it is the understanding of the church which ever reappears in the avant garde at the moments of real church renewal. It is the avant garde and full expression of the church of renewal.

However, this does not mean that it can simply replace the institutional church. The institutional church represents the historical dimension of the church's existence. As such it is a necessary, albeit secondary expression of the church. It is necessary precisely for that dimension of historical perpetuation of the church's message as tradition which continually makes the gospel available to a new generation. By contrast the gathered church of explicit believers cannot perpetuate itself. If it tries to do so, it simply loses itself and becomes another institution. The two are really interdependent polarities within the total dialectic of the church's existence. The charismatic community can be free to be itself when it can resign the work of transmission to the institution and allow itself to form its life and let go of its life only so long as the vital spirit lasts within it. The historical church, in turn, remains vital and is constantly renewed through its ability to take in and absorb the insights of the believer's church. But in order to receive the fruits of the believer's church, it must be willing to accept whatever freedom the believer's church feels is necessary for the flowering of its own experimental spirit. It must be willing to let communities arise autonomously and without any specific kind of institutional ties to work out their own gifts, and yet still to remain in the kind of open communication with these free communities which will allow their fruits to be given to the church as a whole. Only in this way does the whole dialectic of historical Christianity work as it should.[13]

Ruether admits, however, that this dialectic never completely works as it should because of the fallenness of humanity and of the church. "Hence we constantly block the free movement of the dialectic of renewal in the church and fall into alienation and schism." Ruether cautions that unless room is given for this "free church" expression, the Spirit's renewing work "flees outside the bonds of historical Christianity and takes up its work elsewhere."[14]

Our interest is drawn to the structural model Ruether outlines, not the particular examples of renewal, or understandings of what constitutes renewal, which she gives. Also, one might raise questions about the existential-historical dialectic and might wish to argue that the "free church" community is no less historical than the institutional church. Structurally, however, Ruether's model is in essence the same as that proposed by Ralph Winter in calling for a normative "sodality structure" for mission and renewal analogous to the Catholic religious orders,[15] and shows basically what I mean by a mediating model.

Marks of a Mediating Model   Combining elements of both the institutional and the charismatic perspectives, such a model of renewal assumes the fact and the value of some form of the institutional church as well as the need for repeated renewal through more or less distinct renewal movements.

The problem is to conceive of a renewing structure which brings new life to the larger church without either compromising its own vitality or causing a split. It must be a structure which can be seen as normative; that is, whose appearance and impact are seen not as an aberration but as part of the working of the Spirit of God in the church. (This is not to imply that the decline of the church is ever "normative," but only that, given conditions of decline, one may expect certain patterns of renewal.)

The following model appears to fit these requirements. All the elements described below were found in early Methodism and could be illustrated as well from other renewal movements. And this model seems to me to be an elaboration of the way John Wesley himself understood the Spirit's renewing work in the church.

1. *The renewal movement exists as an* ecclesiola. That is, it is a smaller, more intimate expression of the church within the church. It sees itself not as the true church in an exclusive sense, but as a form of the church which is necessary to the life of the larger church, and which in turn needs the larger church in order to be complete. It understands itself as necessary not merely because of a perceived lack in the larger church but also because of a conviction that the Christian faith can be fully experienced only in some such "subecclesial" or small-church form.

2. *The renewing movement uses some form of small group structure.* It is an *ecclesiola* not merely in a vague or general sense, but takes on a specific small group form within the local congregation. Thus it is an *ecclesiola,* not only as a group within the Christian church at large, but also in the more restricted sense of a movement expressing itself in specific small communities within the local congregation. While the size and structure of these small groups may vary, they generally are composed of a dozen or less persons and meet regularly once a week.

3. *The renewal movement has some structural link with the institutional church.* This is crucial if the renewal structure is to exercise a revitalizing impact without bringing division. Some kind of tie between the two structures is mutually sought and agreed upon. This may mean ecclesiastical recognition as a religious order, ordination of renewal leaders or organizational linkage. It may follow the model of official recognition of and liaison with the renewal body, as in the current case of Roman Catholic relations with the Catholic charismatic renewal. It was especially this structural tie which was lacking in the case of Methodism and the Waldenses. Count Zinzendorf sought such a tie, with only limited success, in the case of the Moravians; Francis of Assisi fully achieved one by gaining papal approval for his order.[16]

4. Because it sees itself not as the total church but as a necessary part of the church, *the renewal structure is committed to the unity, vitality and wholeness of the larger church.* It will be concerned first of all with the life of that branch of the church which forms its most immediate context (for example, a denomination or a theological or ecclesiastical tradition), but will also have a vision for the universal church and a concern for its unity and united witness.

5. *The renewal structure is mission-oriented.* It senses keenly its specific purpose and mission, which is conceived in part as the renewal of the church and in part as witness to the world. It will stress practical ethics, attempting to combine faith and love, belief with everyday life.[17]

6. *The renewal movement is especially conscious of being a distinct, covenant-based community.* It knows it is not the whole church; it senses its own incompleteness. But it sees itself as a visible form of the true church. It does not attempt or intend to carry on all the functions of the church but is a restricted community of people voluntarily committed to each other. Based on a well-understood covenant, it has the capability of exercising discipline, even to the point of exclusion, among its members.

As a community the renewal movement prizes face-to-face relationships, mutuality and interdependence. It especially stresses Scriptures which speak of koinonia, mutual encouragement and admonition within the body, and sees itself as a primary structure for experiencing these aspects of the church.

7. *The renewal movement provides the context for the rise, training, and exercise of new forms of ministry and leadership.* Out of its experience of community comes a practical emphasis on the gifts of the Spirit and the priesthood of believers. This consciousness combines with the natural need for leadership within the movement and the outward impulse of witness and service to produce both the opportunity and the enabling

context for new forms of ministry and new leaders who arise not through the more restricted, established ecclesiastical channels (typically, education and ordination), but through practical experience and the shared life of the group. This happened in Methodism as well as in other renewal movements.

The renewal group provides not only opportunities for leadership and service but also a natural environment for training new leaders. Partly for this reason, a disproportionately high number of future church leaders often comes from the ranks of a renewal movement if it is not cut off from the established church.

8. Finally, *the renewal structure maintains an emphasis on the Spirit and the Word as the basis of authority.* It is both Christological and pneumatological. It stresses the norm of Scripture and the life of the Spirit, and maintains both of these in some tension with the traditionalism of the institutional church. If it veers to the right or the left at this point, it will become either a highly legalistic sect or an enthusiastic cult liable to extreme or heretical beliefs. In the case of Methodism, Wesley was able to maintain a balance which prevented either extreme.

The renewal movement stresses the Spirit and the Word as the ultimate ground of authority, but within limits also recognizes the authority and traditions of the institutional church.

In summary, this is a model for renewal which assigns a normative role both to the institutional church and to a movement and structure for renewal. Obviously no actual instance of a renewal movement in an institutional church perfectly fits the model. It is possible, however, that the model could be useful in comparing and evaluating various renewal movements, including contemporary ones.

It is important to note that this model of renewal is capable of including, at least conceptually, not only renewal movements which remain within the institutional church but also the believers' churches or other groups which become independent sects. It can include many of the medieval "heretical" sects, or at least those whose only heresy was to separate from Rome. In the first place, the model provides some help in understanding why such groups do, in fact, become independent. More importantly, if one's understanding of "church" is broad enough to include all the people of God in the various communions, all those who confess Jesus Christ as Savior and Lord, then such independent churches and sects may still be seen as *ecclesiolae* within the church of Christ, even though they are independent of any particular ecclesiastical structure larger than themselves.

One could readily illustrate the points of this model from the histories of Continental Pietism, Moravianism, Methodism, some Catholic religious orders and the charismatic movement, as well as from other movements of the past and present. The pattern emerges with some consistency throughout history. Looking at it systematically as a model clarifies some of the reasons why renewal happens the way it does. And it suggests important points where the flow of renewal can be either choked or strengthened, either by action of the movement itself or by reaction of the larger church body.

I suggest this model both as a useful hypothesis in understanding church renewal and as a resource for those concerned or involved with renewal. The more we can learn from the past to understand the human and divine processes in renewal, the more useful we may be as agents of renewal ourselves.

All this presupposes, however, the recognition at the most fundamental level that God is sovereign and that his Spirit moves in the church in his own time and way. But God tells us not to be like the horse or mule, which have no understanding, but to seek wisdom and knowledge of his ways that we may be useful and willing instruments in his hands. God invites us to cooperate with him in the work of renewal, and his acts in history suggest clues we would do well not to ignore.

11
THE WESLEYAN
SYNTHESIS

According to some critics John Wesley never had an original idea in his life. He just borrowed from others.

Even if true, this would hardly solve the riddle of Wesley. His genius and originality lay precisely in his borrowing, adapting and combining diverse elements into a synthesis more dynamic than the sum of its parts.

The Bible says salvation is all of grace, not of works. It also says we are to work out our own salvation, that faith without works is dead. Wesley's way out of this paradox was through Galatians 5:6—"faith working by love." This became a favorite passage and theme. True faith shed God's love abroad in the heart, which became the fountainhead of "all inward and outward holiness."

Wesley's genius, under God, lay in developing and maintaining a synthesis in doctrine and practice that kept biblical paradoxes paired and powerful. He held together faith and works, doctrine and experience, the individual and the social, the concerns of time and eternity.

It is this synthesis which speaks most profoundly to the church today. In this chapter we will examine the key elements of the Wesleyan synthesis, noting how these tie in to the life and experience of the church.

Divine Sovereignty and Human Freedom   Basic to all else in Wesley was his tenacious hold on both the total sovereignty of God and the freedom of human beings to accept or reject God's call and to cooperate with the Holy Spirit in the work of salvation—both in individual believers and in the world.

Wesley's starting point was not the decrees of God nor the logic required to resolve theological paradoxes. Rather it was what Scripture affirms: God is sovereign; besides him there is no other god; all salvation depends on his initiative and working. But humans, even though sinful, still have a measure of freedom. And if they turn to God, they can be his coworkers in the concerns of the Kingdom.

John Wesley stressed the image of God as well as the Word of God. Human creation in the divine image was fundamental for Wesley because it meant a deep, ineffaceable similarity between the human spirit and the Spirit of God which even the tragic effects of the Fall could not destroy. Salvation was still possible. But only by God's grace, because sin put men and women under such bondage that they could never freely turn to God.

Like Gregory of Nyssa and other early teachers of the Eastern Church, Wesley saw *the will* as essential to the image of God. God had given men and women a will, either to serve him or to rebel. Now, because of sin, the will was under bondage. People chose to do evil rather than good. Salvation therefore meant restoring the image of God and freeing the will to do God's will. By grace, men and women could will to serve God. Thus the highest perfection in Christian experience is to serve God with the whole mind, heart and will. In a passage typical of many others, Wesley says that true Christianity is "the love of God and our neighbour; the image of God stamped on the heart; the life of God in the soul of man; the mind that was in Christ, enabling us to walk as Christ also walked."[1]

The key to Wesley's skill in stressing both God's sovereignty and human freedom was his doctrine of grace, particularly his stress on "prevenient grace." On their own human beings cannot take the smallest step toward God. But God has not left us alone. An unconditional benefit of Christ's atonement is that God maintains the human race in a savable position. God's grace is "prevenient"; that is, it "goes before" (Latin, *praevenire,* to come before, anticipate) us, giving us the capacity, if we will, to turn to God. Yet even this turning is aided by God's grace shed abroad universally in the world by the death and resurrection of Jesus Christ.

John Calvin spoke of common or general grace, that blessing of God in the world which explains how even depraved persons can accomplish commendable (if not morally good) works. But due to Calvin's doctrine of unconditional election, common grace plays no part, finally, in God's plan of redemption. By contrast, Wesley saw prevenient grace as the first step in God's redeeming work, even though people could (and most would) reject this grace. He saw God's grace as "preventing [or coming before], accompanying, and following" every person.[2] Thus God is sovereign and man is free. In Colin Williams's words, with the doctrine of prevenient grace Wesley "broke the chain of logical necessity by which the Calvinist doctrine of predestination seems to flow from the doctrine of original sin."[3]

Because of his emphasis on human freedom and the universality of the atonement, Wesley has often been considered an Arminian, but this is so only in a qualified sense. Methodists "come to the very edge of Calvinism," Wesley said: "(1.) In ascribing all good to the free grace of God. (2.) In denying all natural free-will, and all power antecedent to grace. And, (3.) In excluding all merit from man; even for what he has or does by the grace of God."[4] As George Croft Cell noted, Wesley (in his sermon "Salvation by Faith") "goes as far as Paul, Augustine, Luther or Calvin ever did or could go in pressing to the limit the exclusive causality of God in man's experience of salvation as well as in any and all provisions of redemption."[5] Taking Wesley's whole system into account, it is something of a distortion to speak of "Wesleyan-Arminianism"; one could as truly speak of "Wesleyan-Calvinism."

Wesley was as fully conscious as the earlier Reformers were of God's grace. But he had a deep optimism of grace that formed the foundation for his emphasis on the universal atonement, the witness of the Spirit and Christian perfection. He saw God's grace so fully abounding that one could not set limits on what God's Spirit might accomplish through the church in the present order. Wesley's synthesis thus preserves an important and hopeful role for the church. This view is optimistic as to the moral transformation of human beings (the restoration of the image of God) made possible by grace, and it sees the church as the instrumental means for promoting redemption in personal experience and in society. Wesley's view *takes the church seriously* as an agent of grace in the world. It therefore speaks to the contemporary need to build a more radical and biblical ecclesiology and, especially, a more biblically faithful community of believers.

Doctrine and Experience Because of his dual stress on divine sovereignty and human freedom, Wesley focused on Christian experience. He looked for moral transformation in believers' lives, demonstrated by their behavior.

Thus Wesley stressed both doctrine and experience, once again, "faith working by love." If faith didn't produce moral change, including good works, it wasn't true faith. Thus also Wesley's concern with sanctification: Regeneration began and enabled the process of sanctification, so every believer was morally obligated to "press on to perfection." Justification and sanctification went together. Wesley said of the Methodists

that as they do not think or speak of justification so as to supersede sanctification, so neither do they think or speak of sanctification so as to supersede justification. They take care to keep each in its own place, laying equal stress on one and the other. They know God has joined these together, and it is not for man to put them asunder: Therefore they maintain, with equal zeal and diligence, the doctrine of free, full, present justification, on the one hand, and of entire sanctification both of heart and life, on the other; being as tenacious of inward holiness as any Mystic, and of outward, as any Pharisee.[6]

Wesley's oft-repeated stress on both inward and outward holiness is evidence of this balance of doctrine and experience. An inner experience of God in the soul which does not result in one's "doing all the good you can" is inherently suspect. Wesley's concern for sanctification simply shows he really believed that doctrine and experience go together. Men and women do not truly *believe* the gospel without a moral change which enables them to *live* the gospel. Faith not only believes; it *works*—in both senses.

This balance between doctrine and experience shows itself also in Wesley's dual stress on reason and experience. At the high tide of Deism Wesley stressed that faith was rational and reason was its handmaid. And even when criticized as a mad enthusiast, he still insisted on the conscious sense of God in the soul and on the inner witness of the Spirit.

This balanced emphasis gave Methodism a strong ethical sensitivity. But it also underscored the important role of the church, because Wesley knew the Christian community was either the environment where God's grace turned sinners into saints or else a cold, lifeless shell where newborn believers died of spiritual exposure. Wesley would join those voices in our day calling for the recovery of such a balance.

Experience and Structure   This leads to the aspect of the Wesleyan synthesis with perhaps the greatest potential impact for the church today. *Wesley saw the connection between experience and structure.* Perhaps no one in church history was more keenly aware of the relationship between Christian experience and appropriate nurturing structures, or was so successful in matching church forms to church life. Certainly he was more successful at this point than Luther in Saxony or Calvin in Geneva, or even Zinzendorf in Herrnhut.

Wesley's system of societies, classes and bands in large measure formed the genius of the discipline, growth and enduring impact of Methodism. To these were added many other structures, including schools, dispensaries and loan funds for those in need.

The Methodist system grew out of Wesley's keen awareness of the social nature of Christian experience—the balance of the individual and the community. As early as 1729 a "serious man" whom Wesley sought out told him, "Sir, you wish to serve God and go to heaven? Remember that you cannot serve him alone. You must therefore find companions or make them; the Bible knows nothing of solitary religion."[7] Wesley followed this advice for the next sixty years, always avoiding "solitary religion." This was at the heart of his reservations about mysticism.

When Wesley spoke of "social holiness" and "social Christianity," he was pointing to New Testament koinonia. Christian fellowship meant, not merely corporate worship, but watching over one another in love, advising, exhorting, admonishing and praying with the brothers and sisters.[8] "This, and this alone, is Christian fellowship," he said. And this is what Methodism promoted: "We introduce Christian fellowship where it was utterly destroyed. And the fruits of it have been peace, joy, love, and zeal for every good word and work."[9]

The great instrument for building this quality of community or fellowship was the Methodist system of society, class meeting and band. For Wesley, the class meeting was an ecclesiological statement, integrally linked to sanctification. In Wesley's view, if believers were really serious in their quest for holiness, they would band together in small groups to experience that level of community which is the necessary environment for growth in grace.

Students of Wesley and of spiritual renewal are increasingly coming to see the relevance of Wesley's practical structures, particularly the class meeting.[10] It is ironic that many books on Wesley make only passing reference to the class meeting, even though Wesley himself saw it as in many ways the cornerstone of Methodism. By and large those who advocate Wesleyan theology in our own day have forgotten this practical small group structure and thus have tended to overindividualize Wesley's concept of sanctification and to lose the secret of much of the spiritual power of early Methodism.

Richard Lovelace is surely right in his supposition that the demise of the class meeting in large measure explains the decline of Methodism. Referring to the class meeting Lovelace comments, "It is startling that a strategy as obvious and effective as small groups could be discovered and widely used in recent history and then apparently lost until its modern rediscovery in popular religious movements. A generation of formal Christians intervening between awakenings appears sufficient to erase them from the church's memory."[11]

The implication here for the modern church seems obvious: the recovery of some functional equivalent of the class meeting with its intimacy, mutual care and support, and discipline is essential. Such a rigorous structure naturally goes against the grain in our lax, individualistic, live-and-let-live society. But this is precisely why it is needed. Talk of discipline, discipleship and responsible Christian lifestyle seldom gets beyond mere talk until folks make the kind of serious covenant commitment to each other which provides the structure for space-time follow-through on professed beliefs and shows that believers are willing to ratify their commitment to Christ by commitment to his body. Only thus do we begin to understand *in practice* the truth that "we are members of each other."

The discipline and rigor of the class meeting were no less scandalous in Wesley's day. Wesley saw, however, that such covenant structures were essential if Christians were to make a successful stand against the world, the flesh and the devil and to be gospel leaven in society. In any time when Christian values are in near-total eclipse, only a countercultural expression of the church will have the spiritual and social power to speak a gospel word to the dominant spirit of the age.[12]

The Charismatic and the Institutional   Wesley's balance between the charismatic and the institutional elements in church life and experience has surfaced at various points throughout this book. Some of the practical implications of this aspect of the Wesleyan synthesis were discussed in the last chapter. My point here is to stress that this dual emphasis fits into the larger picture of Wesley's understanding of the church and Christian experience.

The curious thing about early Methodism is that it was a charismatic church within the institutional church. Many point to Methodism's separation from the Church of England as sure proof of the inevitable failure of Wesley's theory and approach. But it is not at all clear either that the final outcome was inevitable or that eventual separation means failure.

Look at the historical circumstances. They are important. Here we face three facts: Wesley was never expelled from the Church of England; he never left or permitted Methodism to do so; and the church never gave Methodism any kind of official status. Had these circumstances been different, the outcome would likely have been different. Since Wesley was never kicked out of or disciplined by the Church of England despite his rather extraordinary innovations, he was able to develop his views and practices in a basically

Anglican way. And since the Methodist societies were never given official status within the Anglican Church, they developed independently, under Wesley, rather than being officially recognized as an evangelical Anglican order. It was this, of course, which eventually led to Methodist separation (over Wesley's dead body) and which left Methodists as ecclesiological orphans. Wesley appears to have hoped, at least early on, that some kind of official recognition for Methodism would be granted by the Anglican authorities. If this had happened, the history of Methodism—and probably of Anglicanism—would have been much different.

The unique features of Wesley's concept of the church thus trace mainly to the peculiar position of Methodism within Anglicanism. If Methodism had arisen within the Roman Church, it might have become a recognized order, Wesley perhaps seeking an accommodation with Pope Benedict XIV. Conversely, if Methodism had been born two centuries earlier within Reformation Protestantism, it would likely have been forced to become a separate believers' church.

It will always be argued (from both sides) that Wesley's institutional-charismatic synthesis is fundamentally inconsistent and impossible. In fact, it is part of the larger synthesis discussed in this chapter. No one needs to affirm that Wesley was totally consistent over the course of half a century, and serious questions can be raised at several points. It seems to me, however, that Wesley's fundamental perspective is essentially sound when viewed biblically, historically and sociologically. The seeming paradoxes in Wesley's views are due not to a fundamental inconsistency but rather to the paradoxical nature of the church in a sinful world, which makes a totally consistent, systematic theory of the church difficult, if not impossible, from a human standpoint. Added to this was Wesley's concern, not to work out a systematic ecclesiology, but rather to understand and explain Methodism as it grew in response to the renewing work of the Holy Spirit.

In maintaining both the charismatic and the institutional dimensions of the church, with the primary accent on the charismatic, the Wesleyan synthesis did not flee from history into pure existentialism but kept the present tied to the past. Methodism sought to be neither above history nor shackled by tradition. This was the basis for Wesley's seeing Methodism as *ecclesiola in ecclesia*—the charismatic community (not entirely unstructured) within the institutional church (not entirely devoid of grace).

Present and Future Salvation   Finally, the Wesleyan synthesis balances present and future salvation. No one can accuse Wesley of underemphasizing eternal blessedness with God. In fact, Wesley's understanding of the Kingdom of God may be too otherworldly and too static. But Wesley's whole stress on sanctification, or Christian perfection, centered in the *present* reality of the life of God in the human soul and was a progressive, dynamic concept. He reasoned that if holiness could come at death, God could just as surely enable holy living now.

And by stressing "all inward and outward holiness" on biblical grounds, Wesley kept Christian experience from retreating into an inner world divorced from the problems and sufferings of daily life. Holiness involved making a present stand for the righteousness of the Kingdom of God and especially bringing the gospel to the poor.

We have noted in chapter seven how Wesley combined the emphases of eschatological hope and final judgment, present and future salvation, and the evangelistic and prophetic dimensions of the gospel. Because salvation is for eternity, Wesley was an evangelist who preached "the wrath to come." Because salvation is for the present, Wesley reached the poor and worked for social reform. This too is evidence of the Wesleyan synthesis. And it suggests the task set before the church today.

12
WESLEY AND
THE CHURCH TODAY

Two tasks remain. In this final chapter I wish to make a biblical critique of some aspects of Wesley's perspective, then to draw together several strands which are especially important for our experience in the church today.

A Biblical Critique Every major figure in the drama of God's plan of salvation has suffered much at the hands of his or her friends. Like the Corinthian believers, God's people begin to call themselves after the name of one or another of God's apostles, forming feuding factions. One of the reasons for this is that later generations in a religious movement fail to keep the original leader's breadth of insight. They tend to focus on one or two points rather than maintaining the balance and breadth of the whole gospel.

Now we see "darkly" and partially. We fail to see the whole picture, and even when we see it, we betray part of it in practice. Inevitably, it seems, we wander at least a few degrees to the right or left. Part of the Spirit's renewing work in history is to correct the course of the church, bringing it back to the recovery of neglected biblical truth.

So it is with John Wesley. He recovered a biblical balance at several key points. In the providence of God and the course of history he was uniquely placed to combine in himself and in early Methodism truths and insights which seldom in church history have been found together in such creative tension.

We must insist that our source, however, is Jesus Christ, Lord of the church, uniquely revealed in Scripture. We dare to follow Wesley, Luther, Calvin or anyone else only to the extent that they follow Jesus. The church's task in every age is not only to learn from God's works in history but also to continually subject history to the norm of the biblical revelation.

Throughout this book we have noticed the points at which John Wesley rediscovered biblical themes or sustained a balance between seemingly contradictory truths. There are points, however, where biblical questions need to be raised about Wesley's understanding of the church.

It seems to me that Wesley's affirmation of both the institutional and charismatic dimensions of the church and Christian experience is true both to biblical and postbiblical history. I would make no major critique of his understanding of Christian experience, the corporate life of the church or fundamental Christian doctrine. Others approaching Wesley from different theological perspectives and traditions will, of course, disagree at some of these points.

I would, however, mount three criticisms that tie in especially with the theme of this book. These concern Wesley's understanding of ministry, his social and political outlook, and his view of the Kingdom of God.

1. *Wesley's View of Ministry.* For an age which was nervous about anything having to do with spiritual gifts or a direct experience of the Holy Spirit (labeled "enthusiasm"), Wesley's openness to the gifts of the Spirit was remarkable. Ever the ardent experientialist, Wesley was always watching to see what God would do next and was disposed to see God at work in unconventional ways and unexpected places. Noting that God

blessed his own preaching more because of Aldersgate than Oxford, he was able to see that God was ready and willing to work through unusual channels and unordained preachers.

As Wesley's ministry developed and he began commissioning a whole regiment of traveling preachers, two options were open to him to explain biblically what was happening. One would have been a radical affirmation of the doctrine of the priesthood of believers, an assertion that biblically and in God's plan every believer is called to minister and that the various forms of ministry are based on the charismatic work of the Holy Spirit rather than on the institutional accreditation of the church. The other option, which Wesley essentially took, was to admit the normal validity of ecclesiastical ordination but to see the Holy Spirit as breaking through this mold and creating an "extraordinary" pattern of ministry in a fashion outside but somewhat parallel to normal ecclesiastical structures.

These two options may not really be mutually exclusive. As noted, Wesley did incorporate the charismatic emphasis to some extent. On the other hand, it seems to me that Wesley did not go far enough in this direction. He did not sufficiently stress the revolutionary implications of the priesthood of believers and the gifts of the Spirit for the ministry of the church.

It is clear that Wesley's extraordinary-ordinary distinction regarding gifts and offices in the church was functionally important to his view of ministry. The church has an "ordinary," ecclesiastically accredited ordained ministry. But because of the fallen nature of the church the Holy Spirit from time to time must break through this encrusted structure and create an "extraordinary" ministry for renewing the church. The problem, as we have noted, is that this is not a biblical distinction. It does not erase the unbiblical clergy-laity split but simply in effect redefines and broadens the clergy category. Thus when Methodism later separated from

Anglicanism, Wesley's lay preachers simply became the Methodist clergy, and for more than half a century laymen had no effective voice within the Methodist structure. Partly in protest, the Free Methodists and other groups from their beginning provided for equal lay and clergy representation in church government. But of course this also did not get to the core of the problem.

The biblical understanding of ministry combines the priesthood of believers, the gifts of the Spirit, and the fact that all believers are servants and ministers of Jesus Christ. The clergy or "professional religionist" category is wiped out; the priesthood is expanded to include all believers under the high priesthood of Jesus Christ. The fullness of grace found in Jesus is apportioned to the whole body so that each believer receives one or more spiritual gifts for the common good. So the New Testament differentiation is not between ministers and laymen, but between varieties of ministries flowing from the gracious work of the Spirit. The equipping ministries (apostle, prophet, evangelist, pastor, teacher) do not constitute "the ministry" or a new hierarchy, but function to equip the whole body for ministry. All of this is clearly taught in 1 Corinthians 12, Ephesians 1—4, 1 Peter and elsewhere.

What would have happened had Wesley seen his preachers and other helpers in this more fully biblical way? For one thing, he probably would have been even more open to commissioning a wide variety of ministers, including women, in Methodism. On the other hand, he might have become even more embroiled in controversy because he would have been seen as undercutting the very institution of the clergy. Clergymen, like all professionals, very quickly take on the mentality of a closed club and have sensitive antennae for picking up any threats to their clerical status and privileges.

I am convinced, however, that a more fully biblical view of ministry would have been compatible with Wesley's ecclesiology. It would have given him a more consistent and thoroughly biblical theory of the church and would have strengthened both his ecclesiology and the enduring dynamic of the Methodist movement.

The practical implication of this for today is the need to affirm the New Testament view of ministry and make structural provision for implementing it. This should not be threatening to ordained ministers if they concentrate on their proper calling as enablers and equippers and on the particular gifts God has granted them. This is, in fact, the way to escape the frustration of trying to be all things to all people.

2. *Social and Political Outlook.* We have seen that Wesley was a political and religious conservative who only gradually changed his views because of what he saw God doing in experience. It seems that Wesley changed his opinions more regarding the church than regarding politics and the state. This is understandable since the church was his primary sphere of activity. He remained an ardent monarchist and political conservative in the face of more democratic currents.

For this reason Wesley does not make a good guide on social and political questions, nor consequently on questions of the social, political and economic implications of the gospel. The Anabaptists developed their views on pacifism and the role of the state partly because they were forced outside of a political-ecclesiastical system which could not stand the idea of separation between church and state. Two hundred years later, Wesley was the heir of the toleration which developed in large measure because of the impact of the Radical Reformation and the believers' churches. Had he run afoul of the government and the law in the same manner that he clashed with church tradition, he might well have become as radical in his politics and his social ethics as he became in his understanding of the church. This does not, of course, answer the question as to what a biblically sound social and political perspective would look like.

All this is a way of saying that Wesley developed an essentially sound and biblical understanding of the nature of Christian discipleship and the church but failed to think through the social and political implications of such a vision. Without attempting to argue here for any particular socio-ethical understanding of the gospel, I would suggest at least that a more thoroughgoing and biblical investigation of this question is needed today than Wesley was forced or able to make.

For example, consider Wesley's reaction to the industrialization of England. He had deep compassion for the laboring victims of this emerging system and worked for its humanization, but he made no fundamental critique of the free enterprise system. A century later in England, Karl Marx did, but unfortunately with a non-Christian bias. It has been said that the Wesleyan Revival saved England from political revolution. Is it possible that a more radical social ethic in Methodism could have saved the world from the Communist revolution a century and a half later by making it unnecessary? One wonders.[1]

Some will argue, of course, that Wesley's political and religious views were inextricably and necessarily connected. I would argue rather that the trajectory of Wesley's whole life was toward a biblical world view, but that he made greater progress in the area of the church and Christian experience than in the social and political realm. In many ways he was ahead of his time even in this area, however, as seen most clearly in his vigorous opposition to the institution of slavery.

If this perspective is valid, it means we do not have to buy into Wesley's social and political views in order to appreciate his ecclesiology. Rather, given his understanding of the church (to the degree it is biblical), the present task is to understand and incarnate the social, political and economic implications of that view.

3. *The Kingdom of God.* A progressive, dynamic understanding of salvation underlies all of John Wesley's thought.

This is seen particularly in his doctrine of grace and his understanding of sanctification, which in Wesley is much more dynamic than in many of his later interpreters.

Nevertheless, one detects a tension between the static and dynamic elements in Wesley's understanding of salvation. Even though he saw sanctification as in one sense dynamic and progressive, he was not entirely free of the classical Greek notion of perfection as changelessness and salvation as the attainment of an eternal blessedness which is essentially static.

This is evident at times when Wesley speaks of the Kingdom of God. Frequently for Wesley the Kingdom of God is "righteousness, peace, and joy in the Holy Spirit."[2] It is, fundamentally, the direct experience of God through Jesus Christ. Wesley was quick to stress the present implications of the gospel and the requirement of the obedience of good works, as we have noted. But underlying this seems to be the suspicion that the only real significance of good works and of the present life is their function in preparing us for eternity, conceived in somewhat static terms.

One must walk a careful line here. The final goal of salvation in Scripture does involve eternal life in the immediate presence of God, and certainly our present experience of the gospel loses all ultimate meaning if this eternal dimension is lost sight of. But in Scripture even eternal existence is seen in dynamic rather than static terms, and no absolute discontinuity is drawn between present life and history and the final culmination of the Kingdom of God. Time is more than just the dressing room for eternity. It has meaning and purpose as the arena of God's present activity and as the playing field for the history-long struggle between the Kingdom of God and the kingdom of darkness. And the final victory of God's Kingdom in some way involves the created order.

This is not to make a fundamental criticism of Wesley,

but rather to point out a tendency. Certainly the dialectic between time and eternity, between process and stasis, runs throughout Wesley's thought. But perhaps Wesley's immersion in the early Greek and medieval Christian tradition kept him from being fully biblical at this point, with the result that Wesley's understanding of the Kingdom of God did not give sufficient weight and meaning to the work and witness of the church in the temporal order. The implications here tie in with the matters discussed above regarding the social and political meaning of the gospel.

What does all this mean for the life and experience of the church today? Primarily that we must determine our understanding of the Kingdom of God and of the church's agency in the Kingdom on the basis of the biblical revelation. The body of Christ is to be an eschatological and messianic community of the Kingdom in a more fundamentally important sense than Wesley understood.

And so we come back to the question of the life and witness of the Christian community, the church.

The Shape of the Church   John Wesley was nothing if not practical. He demonstrated that a high standard of Christian perfection was intensely practical. Both his understanding of the church and the experience of early Methodism speak pointedly to the life of the people of God today.

In concluding this study, we may summarize the main points at which Wesley's understanding of the church speaks most potently to our present situation. It seems to me that the following points speak with special seriousness to a biblically faithful recovery of the life of the church.

1. *The church must exercise discipline based on a covenant commitment to Christian community.* A personal commitment to Jesus Christ as Lord and Savior must be tied to a covenant commitment to the body of Christ. Believers must be ready to take some agreed responsibility for their own lives and for

the lives of their sisters and brothers in the faith.

Commitment to Christ, no matter how sincere, has a way of evaporating with time if not tied to and reinforced by specific commitments and disciplines which undergird the corporate experience of the Christian community. This kind of commitment is necessary if the body of Christ is to live and maintain the values of the Kingdom of God within an antagonistic cultural environment. Only a covenant community can give effective witness to the Kingdom. Only a covenant community has the sociological strength to be a Christian counterculture in a deteriorating hedonistic society.

Some people are understandably reluctant to set specific disciplines or covenant commitments for fear of legalism and of establishing nonbiblical barriers to faith or to entrance into the church. How can the church, for instance, require certain lifestyle patterns which are not prescribed in the Bible?

The answer to this objection is twofold. First, corporate disciplines should not be equated with salvation itself. This often amounts to undercutting salvation by faith and confusing justification with sanctification. Discipline has the relationship to justification that works have to faith: it is the necessary and natural expression of a genuine encounter with God.

Secondly, discipline and covenant commitment are most effectively and wholesomely expressed at the level of the *ecclesiola*, the small group. In the case of Methodism, this commitment and discipline functioned at the level of the classes and bands. It seems that only at this level can discipline operate in an organic and spiritually vital, rather than institutional and legalistic, way.

The fundamental fact here is that the church is always a voluntary community. But this is the church's strength, not its weakness. The whole idea of covenant is based on willing commitment. It is this covenant commitment which makes discipline possible. Because the commitment is earnest and serious, the covenant provides for excluding from the committed community those who flagrantly violate the covenant, those Wesley styled "disorderly walkers." People enter the covenant community, in effect, by contract. The parties agree that the violation of the contract is cause for exclusion and separation. Since the covenant is willingly entered into, exclusion or excommunication for violation of the covenant is not unjust or arbitrary. It is seen not as an institutional act but as a necessary consequence of the violation of a trust. And when such discipline operates at the level of small groups or ecclesial subcommunities functioning within a broad concept of the universal church, such exclusion is not necessarily a judgment about final salvation.

2. *The church needs normative structures for community, discipline and mission.* Such structures may not assume the specific forms of the bands or classes, but however they are structured they should exercise the same basic functions.

The whole tenor of this book suggests the need for some sort of committed small group structures for the vitality and renewal of the larger church. The discussion of the book has, I believe, indicated some of the dynamics involved in the life and structure of such groups and in their relationship to the larger body of Christ.

This is not to suggest that small group structures should be directly patterned after the class or band meetings. But it is to suggest the need for something more than merely fellowship, study or prayer groups. The Methodist system shows the need for covenant, discipline and accountability within the group, and accountability of the group to the larger church body.

The argument Wesley and later Methodists (such as Henry Fish, quoted in chapter five) employed for such structures seems to me unanswerable. It is a simple one: While such groups are not prescribed in Scripture, a level of Christian lifestyle *is* prescribed which fails to materialize without some form of small group structure. Some of the Scriptures which are particularly pointed in this connection, and which have become meaningless to much of the contemporary church, are James 5:16; Hebrews 3:12-13 and 10:24-25; 1 Thessalonians 5:11; Colossians 3:16; Romans 12:15; and Matthew 18:15-18. These behaviors are lost to the church when it does not meet with sufficient frequency, intimacy and commitment to let them develop.

3. *The Wesleyan experience shows that the biblical emphasis on the priesthood of believers and the gifts of the Spirit is entirely practical and workable.* Even (or perhaps especially) among the poor, a sizeable proportion of Christian believers can become effective leaders and ministers provided the vision and appropriate structures are present. All believers can be functioning members of the body. But this requires structures which provide the context for spiritual growth and opportunities for developing leadership. The insight that the Christian ministry is entrusted to the whole body of Christ is not just a nice theory. It works when the body functions biblically.

The experience of John Wesley shows what most Christians suspect: that the essential qualifications for effective, redemptive ministry have little if anything to do with formal education or ecclesiastical status and everything to do with spiritual growth, maturity and structural flexibility. On the other hand, Wesley would not tolerate incompetence. He worked hard at training his helpers and traveling preachers. He practiced theological education by extension two centuries before anyone thought up the name. Preachers carried books and pamphlets for themselves and for others. They were expected constantly to "improve the time" by up to six hours daily in study. In addition, Wesley seldom traveled alone; he often took one or more helpers with him so they could observe and learn from him. He listened to his helpers preach and gave them his criticism and advice.

4. *Wesley's experience shows the value of holding out before the church a high ideal of what God's grace can accomplish in personal experience and in the present order.* The high and dynamic ideal of Christian perfection functioned within Methodism to sustain hope and optimism in the present life and served as a spur toward discipline and toward a high moral and ethical quest. To a large degree, Wesley saw the Kingdom of God in terms of Christian perfection. Such a high idealism, firmly based in Scripture and combining the sanctification and Kingdom themes, is urgently needed in the present experience of the church.

5. *Wesley's experience shows also the importance of the church being in some sense a sacramental community.* Particularly when the body of believers feels the tension between the institutional and charismatic dimensions, and between the present and future dimensions of the Kingdom of God, it needs the continuing reconciling experience of the sense of sacrament. This comes to its fullest expression now in the frequent observance of the Lord's Supper. In this communion believers come to sense and experience at a deeply symbolic level the sacramental or sign nature of the Kingdom community.

We have noted Wesley's strong emphasis on the Lord's Supper and his practice of "constant communion."[3] He strongly urged this upon his people. Constant use of the means of grace was to be the way to spiritual growth and vitality for Methodists. Even though with time Methodists lost much of this sacramental sense, the emphasis still remains valid.

Conclusion We now come to the end of our exploration of John Wesley and his view of the church. Much has been left unsaid. Many points could be explored in greater depth, both with reference to Wesley and his day and with reference to Scripture. I have restricted the discussion to tracing a broad perspective, zeroing in on questions of special import for the shape of our Christian life together.

We have spoken of radicality and synthesis. A synthesis, one could argue, is not very exciting. Synthesis sounds like stew, all the ingredients boiled down to one flavor. This is, in fact, the stale blandness of the *via media,* the middle-of-the-road. The radical extremes, by contrast, excite and invite.

Wesley would argue, however, for a different brand of radicality, neither the one-way extreme nor the boring balance of the middle road. The Wesleyan synthesis is valid to the extent it points to the biblical economy or *oikonomia* of God, which recognizes that the only way to the Kingdom is the mystery and wonder and spiritual ecology of God's plan of redemption.

Basic to God's economy "which he accomplished in Jesus Christ," head of the church, is the life and witness of the Christian community, the church. John Wesley was a radical Christian precisely because radical Christianity is not a system of doctrine but the experience of the body of Christ as a community of discipleship. Wesley learned what radical Christians today are beginning to stress: a really effective struggle for social justice begins with building a biblically faithful community of Christian disciples.

What the world needs now is not Radical Protestantism but radical Christianity. In two thousand years the church has not noticeably improved on the gospel or on the biblical picture of Christian community and discipleship. One of the clearest lessons from twenty centuries of experience is that the church has always been most faithful when it has gotten back to its biblical, spiritual roots. Then it is freed to be most creative in challenging the spiritual, social and economic crises of the day.

This is the meaning of the radical Wesley.

Notes

Preface

[1]Quoted in *The Wittenburg Door* (August-September 1979), p. 29.

[2]Sermon, "Of Former Times," *The Works of John Wesley*, ed. Thomas Jackson (London: John Mason, 1829-31), VII, 165 (hereafter cited as *Works*).

[3]As represented, for instance, by Robert E. Webber, *Common Roots: A Call to Evangelical Maturity* (Grand Rapids: Zondervan, 1978); Robert E. Webber and Donald Bloesch, *The Orthodox Evangelicals* (Nashville: Thomas Nelson, 1978); Peter E. Gillquist, *The Physical Side of Being Spiritual* (Grand Rapids: Zondervan, 1979).

Introduction

[1]*The Journal of the Rev. John Wesley, A.M.*, ed. Nehemiah Curnock (London: Epworth, 1909-16; rpt. 1938), III, 14 (hereafter cited as *Journal*).

[2]Ibid.

[3]Luke Tyerman, *The Life and Times of the Rev. John Wesley, M. A., Founder of the Methodists*, 2nd ed. (London: Hodder and Stoughton, 1876), I, 385-87; A. Skevington Wood, *The Burning Heart: John Wesley, Evangelist* (Grand Rapids: Eerdmans, 1967), pp. 111-12.

[4]Charles W. Ferguson, *Organizing to Beat the Devil: Methodists and the Making of America* (Garden City, New York: Doubleday, 1971).

[5]Letter from Dublin, June 20, 1789, *The Letters of the Rev. John Wesley, A.M.*, ed. John Telford (London: Epworth, 1931), VIII, 145 (hereafter cited as *Letters*).

[6]Ronald A. Knox, *Enthusiasm: A Chapter in the History of Religion* (London: Oxford Univ. Press, 1950), p. 423; Robert G. Tuttle, Jr., *John Wesley: His Life and Theology* (Grand Rapids: Zondervan, 1978), p. 261.

[7]Robert G. Wearmouth, *Methodism and the Common People of the Eighteenth Century* (London: Epworth, 1945), pp. 177-78. John S. Simon, *John Wesley: The Last Phase* (London: Epworth, 1934), p. 319. According to Bernard Semmel, the population of England and Wales grew from an estimated 5,826,000 in 1700 to about 9,156,000 at the end of the century—Bernard Semmel, *The Methodist Revolution* (New York: Basic Books, 1973), p. 9.

[8]C. E. Vulliamy, *John Wesley* (New York: Scribner, 1932), p. vii.

[9]Alan R. Tippett, "The Church Which Is His Body," *Missiology*, 2, No. 2 (April 1974), 147.

[10]But note Wesley's sermons 59 to 69 (or 54 to 64 in some lists), beginning with "On Eternity" and ending with "The New Creation," which give something of a history of redemption.

[11]See J. Gordon Melton, "An Annotated Bibliography of Publications about the Life and Work of John Wesley, 1791-1966," *Methodist History*, 7 (July 1969), 29-46.

[12]A. Skevington Wood, "The Contribution of John Wesley to the Theology of

Grace," in Clark Pinnock, ed., *Grace Unlimited* (Minneapolis: Bethany Fellowship, 1975), p. 209.

[13]Wes Michaelson, "Evangelicalism and Radical Discipleship," in C. Norman Kraus, ed., *Evangelicalism and Anabaptism* (Scottdale, Pa.: Herald Press, 1979), pp. 68-69.

[14]Franklin H. Littell, *The Anabaptist View of the Church* (Boston: Starr King Press, 1952). Later editions have been published with the title *The Origins of Sectarian Protestantism.*

[15]Frank Baker, *John Wesley and the Church of England* (Nashville: Abingdon, 1970), p. 299 (hereafter cited as *JWCE*).

[16]F. Ernest Stoeffler, "Tradition and Renewal in the Ecclesiology of John Wesley," in Bernd Jaspert and Rudolf Mohr, eds., *Traditio–Krisis–Renovatio aus theologischer Sicht* (Marburg: N. G. Elwert, 1976), p. 300.

[17]Ernest A. Payne, *The Free Church Tradition in the Life of England,* 3rd ed. rev. (London: SCM Press, 1951), p. 13.

[18]Donald F. Durnbaugh, *The Believers' Church: The History and Character of Radical Protestantism* (New York: Macmillan, 1968). Durnbaugh has an extensive discussion of the meaning of "believers' church," a term which he prefers to "free church" because of the wide variety of meanings which have been given to the latter term.

[19]Littell, *The Origins of Sectarian Protestantism* (New York: Macmillan, 1964), p. 14.

[20]Leonard Verduin, *The Reformers and Their Stepchildren* (Grand Rapids: Eerdmans, 1964), p. 196. See also below, pp. 114-15, 135-36.

[21]See, for example, George H. Williams, "A People in Community: Historical Background," in James L. Garrett, Jr., ed., *The Concept of the Believers' Church* (Scottdale, Pa.: Herald Press, 1969), pp. 97-142.

Chapter 1

[1]Samuel Wesley, John's father, was rector of the Epworth parish, about one hundred miles north of London. Like John's mother, Susannah, Samuel was a convert to Anglicanism from a Dissenting family.

[2]*Journal,* I, 467.

[3]Vulliamy, p. 23.

[4]Ibid., p. 30. The influence of Law should not be overemphasized, however, for Wesley was simultaneously reading many other books. Also, Wesley from the beginning had a decidedly practical bent which kept him from extreme mysticism. For Wesley's correspondence with Law during the critical month of May 1738, see *Letters,* I, 238-44; John Telford, *The Life of John Wesley* (New York: Phillips and Hunt, 1899), pp. 103-6; Tyerman, I, 185-88. See also J. Brazier Green, *John Wesley and William Law* (London: Epworth, 1945).

[5]Vulliamy, p. 53.

[6]Ibid., p. 60. Later Wesley said he was too concerned at this period for his own soul.

[7]Vulliamy, pp. 53-54; Tyerman, I, 70-72.

[8]John Henry Overton, *Life in the English Church (1660-1714)* (London: Long-

mans, Green, and Co., 1885), pp. 207-9; Arthur W. Nagler, *Pietism and Methodism* (Nashville: Publishing House M. E. Church, South, 1918), pp. 147-48; F. Ernest Stoeffler, "Pietism, the Wesleys, and Methodist Beginnings in America," in F. Ernest Stoeffler, ed., *Continental Pietism and Early American Christianity* (Grand Rapids: Eerdmans, 1976), pp. 185-88.

[9] The relationship between Pietism and the religious society movement (and between Pietism and Methodism) has been mostly ignored. It is significant for Methodism in part because of the close historical interconnections between Pietism and the Moravians. Interestingly, "religious society" and *collegium pietatis* are roughly synonymous designations.

[10] Overton, p. 210; R. Denny Urlin, *John Wesley's Place in Church History* (London: Rivingtons, 1870), p. 15.

[11] Josiah Woodward, *Account of the Rise and Progress of the Religious Societies,* quoted in Overton, p. 211.

[12] Richard P. Heitzenrater, "John Wesley and the Oxford Methodists, 1725-35," Diss. Duke University 1972, pp. 9, 8.

[13] Overton, pp. 211-12; Heitzenrater, pp. 9, 19-23; Martin Schmidt, *John Wesley, A Theological Biography,* II/2, trans. Denis Inman (Nashville: Abingdon, 1973), pp. 175-76. On the subject of the religious societies, see also John S. Simon, *John Wesley and the Religious Societies* (London: Epworth, 1921).

[14] Quoted in Heitzenrater, p. 20.

[15] Ibid., p. 21. The evidence seems to suggest, however, that Samuel Wesley was unsuccessful in carrying out this ambitious program.

[16] Quoted in Heitzenrater, p. 22.

[17] John Whitehead, *The Life of the Rev. John Wesley, M. A.* (London: Stephen Couchman, 1793; Boston: Dow and Jackson, 1845), pp. 38-42. Whitehead, Wesley's personal physician and first biographer, quotes extensively from Susannah Wesley's letters to her husband.

[18] Ibid., pp. 41-42.

[19] Vulliamy, p. 55.

[20] Ibid., pp. 48-49.

[21] Matthew Simpson, *Cyclopedia of Methodism* (Philadelphia: Everts and Stewart, 1878), p. 587; Urlin, p. 16. The word has an interesting history. See Albert M. Lyles, *Methodism Mocked: The Satiric Reaction to Methodism in the Eighteenth Century* (London: Epworth, 1960), p. 22; *The Compact Edition of the Oxford English Dictionary* (New York: Oxford Univ. Press, 1971), I, 1784. In the seventeenth century "Methodists" appears to have been applied also to certain Roman Catholics in their controversies with Protestants. Some reminiscence of this use may lie behind the charges that Wesley was a papist. See Frederick C. Wright, "On the Origin of the Name Methodist," *Proceedings of the Wesley Historical Society,* 3, No. 1 (1901), 10-13.

[22] Vulliamy, p. 54.

[23] Quoted in Heitzenrater, p. 328.

[24] R. Denny Urlin, *The Churchman's Life of Wesley* (London: SPCK, 1905), p. 27; Tyerman, I, 114. Heitzenrater, however, indicates that Wesley went to Georgia "without pay or specific appointment" (p. 329). In fact Wesley set sail before

arrangements were worked out with the SPG but later was allotted the stipend of the man he replaced, the Rev. Mr. Samuel Quincy. The SPG had been organized in 1701 as an offshoot of the SPCK, which came into being in 1698. These two Anglican societies, as well as the Society for the Reformation of Manners, all grew out of the religious society movement previously mentioned. Wesley himself had joined the SPCK in 1732—Heitzenrater, pp. 9, 170; Richard Green, *John Wesley* (London: Charles H. Kelly, n.d.), p. 32. Heitzenrater notes, "The importance of this relationship cannot be exaggerated, for the SPCK was not only a major factor in promoting John Wesley's interest in the Georgia colony, but also was an important source for the suggestion and supply of books for the Oxford Methodists in the years ahead" (p. 170).

[25]Benjamin Ingham's Journal, quoted in Tyerman, I, 121.

[26]Tyerman, I, 120.

[27]*Journal*, I, 142.

[28]Baker, *JWCE*, p. 52.

[29]Ibid., p. 51. I should also point out here that I use the term *lay* reluctantly. For historical reasons, it has been necessary to speak here and elsewhere of "lay ministry," but such terminology contributes to a false clergy-laity dichotomy. Removing this kind of term from our vocabularies might contribute significantly to our rethinking the nature of the church. See Howard A. Snyder, *The Community of the King* (Downers Grove, Ill.: InterVarsity Press, 1977), p. 185, and the critique of Wesley's view of ministry in chapter twelve of this book.

[30]Ibid., p. 44.

[31]Ibid., pp. 51-52.

[32]Richard Butterworth, "Wesley as the Agent of the S.P.G.," *Proceedings of the Wesley Historical Society,* VII, No. 5 (March 1910), 101.

[33]Ibid., p. 102.

[34]Arriving in Georgia, Wesley was required to care for the Anglican parish in Savannah before starting any mission work with the Indians. Although he had some preliminary contact with Indians, he was unable to begin any missionary work.

Chapter 2

[1]John Holmes, *History of the Protestant Church of the United Brethren* (London: J. Nisbet, 1825), I, 308-9.

[2]Ibid., p. 309.

[3]A. J. Lewis, *Zinzendorf the Ecumenical Pioneer* (Philadelphia: Westminster, 1962), p. 125.

[4]Durnbaugh, p. 51.

[5]Ibid., pp. 51-63. See Wesley's *Journal,* II, 28-49 for details of the migration to Germany.

[6]William G. Addison, *The Renewed Church of the United Brethren 1722-1930* (London: SPCK, 1932), p. 51. See also Wesley's *Journal,* II, 28-56.

[7]*Journal*, I, 436-37.

[8]Ibid., II, 60; Holmes, I, 311; Addison, p. 62; Nolan B. Harmon, ed., *The Encyclo-*

pedia of World Methodism (Nashville: United Methodist Publishing House, 1974), pp. 138-39. Halévy notes that Böhler "had been ordained a priest by Zinzendorf the previous year, and since the Church of England had formally recognized the validity of the Moravian episcopacy, John and Charles Wesley did not have the scruples" about him they would otherwise have had. Elie Halévy, *The Birth of Methodism in England,* trans. Bernard Semmel. (Chicago: Univ. of Chicago Press, 1971), p. 55.

[9]Telford, *Life of Wesley,* pp. 95-96.

[10]*Journal,* I, 442.

[11]Ibid., pp. 448-49. Wesley had earlier experimented some with extempore prayer, particularly in services on shipboard, and had witnessed the practice among other groups.

[12]Addison, p. 62.

[13]*Journal,* I, 458.

[14]Wood, *The Burning Heart,* p. 67, quoting Dorothy Marshall.

[15]*Journal,* I, 476.

[16]Harmon, I, 1185; Vulliamy, p. 85; Addison, p. 83; Joseph E. Hutton, *A Short History of the Moravian Church* (London: Moravian Publication Office, 1895), pp. 183-85. Hutton published several books for Wesley.

[17]Addison, p. 83; *Journal,* I, 475, n. 1.

[18]John C. Bowmer, *The Sacrament of the Lord's Supper in Early Methodism* (London: Dacre Press, 1951), p. 38.

[19]*Journal,* I, 458.

[20]Simon, *John Wesley and the Religious Societies,* pp. 196-200; Richard Watson, *The Life of the Rev. John Wesley, A.M.* (New York: Carlton and Phillips, 1853), p. 52. Simon gives the complete rules on pp. 196-98, as does Daniel Benham in *Memoirs of James Hutton* (London: Hamilton, Adams, and Co., 1856), pp. 29-32.

[21]*Journal,* I, 458-59. Vulliamy says, "Here is the germ of Methodist organization, and it cannot be doubted that the rules were drawn up by Wesley himself" (p. 85).

[22]Addison, p. 82.

[23]*Journal,* I, 482.

[24]Stoeffler, "Tradition and Renewal in the Ecclesiology of John Wesley," p. 305.

[25]Ibid., p. 306.

[26]Wesley greatly admired Francke and the Halle institutions. August Francke had died some eleven years earlier, in 1727. Zinzendorf had been a student under him at Halle, 1710-16. Wesley actually visited Halle twice, on July 26-27 and on August 18-19, on the return trip from Herrnhut. Some Moravians later thought Prof. Francke prejudiced Wesley against the Moravians. Wesley also visited Jena (August 20-21) where Böhler and other Moravian and Pietist leaders had studied (*Journal,* II, 16-17, 57-61).

[27]*Journal,* II, 70.

[28]*Works,* XII, 55.

[29]Albert C. Outler, ed., *John Wesley* (New York: Oxford Univ. Press, 1964), p. 353.

[30]*Journal,* II, 121-22, 125.

[31]Ibid., p. 156.

Chapter 3
[1]Harmon, I, 329.
[2]Simon, *John Wesley and the Religious Societies,* p. 271.
[3]Vulliamy, p. 90.
[4]Harris and Griffith Jones, an Anglican "missionary" to Wales, had already begun open-air preaching before 1738. Halévy notes that Whitefield met Jones and Harris soon after his return from America. Whitefield wrote of Harris, "When I first saw him, my Heart was Knit closely to him. I wanted to catch some of his Fire, and gave him the right Hand of Fellowship with my whole heart." Halévy adds, "It was then that Whitefield began open-air preaching near Bristol among the miners of Kingswood, in the manner of the Welsh preachers" (p. 61).
[5]Halévy, p. 69.
[6]Semmel, p. 13.
[7]*The Gentleman's Magazine,* 9 (May 1739), 257.
[8]"Of the pernicious Nature and Tendency of Methodism," *The Gentleman's Magazine,* 9 (May 1739), 257.
[9]*Journal,* II, 167.
[10]Ibid., p. 168.
[11]Ibid., pp. 172-73.
[12]Payne, pp. 92-93; Vulliamy, p. 94.
[13]*John Bennet's Copy of the Minutes of 1744, 1745, 1747, and 1748; with Wesley's Copy of Those for 1746,* Publications of the Wesley Historical Society, No. 1 (London: Charles H. Kelly, 1896), p. 15.
[14]*Works,* VIII, 248-68.
[15]Ibid., p. 250.
[16]Halévy, pp. 42-43.
[17]*Works,* VIII, 250.
[18]Baker, *JWCE,* p. 141.
[19]*Works,* VIII, 258.
[20]"Rules of the Band-Societies," ibid., pp. 272-73. Additional directions were given six years later; ibid., pp. 273-74.
[21]Ibid., pp. 252-53; Watson, p. 96.
[22]*Works,* VIII, 253.
[23]Ibid., p. 253.
[24]Ibid., p. 254.
[25]Wood, pp. 191-92.
[26]"Minutes of Several Conversations . . . ," *Works,* VIII, 307.
[27]*Works,* VIII, 263.

Chapter 4
[1]Holmes, I, 311-12.
[2]Benham, pp. 42-44, 52-53.
[3]Holmes, I, 311; Harmon, II, 1654.
[4]Bowmer, p. 39.
[5]*Journal,* II, 313.
[6]Ibid., p. 314.

[7]Ibid., p. 327.

[8]Ibid., p. 328.

[9]Benham, pp. 46-47.

[10]Ibid., p. 53.

[11]Vulliamy, p. 102; Harmon, II, 1444-45; Tyerman, I, 214, 271-73.

[12]*Journal,* II, 319n.

[13]Frank Baker, "The People Called Methodists. 3. Polity," in Rupert Davies and Gordon Rupp, eds., *A History of the Methodist Church in Great Britain* (London: Epworth, 1965), I, 220.

[14]Knox, p. 472.

[15]Addison, p. 84; Vulliamy, p. 140; Bowmer, p. 39; Holmes, I, 314; and Wesley's *Journal,* II, 370.

[16]*Journal,* II, 371.

[17]Addison, pp. 86-91.

[18]Knox, p. 474; Holmes, I, 315; Harmon, II, 2222; Lewis, pp. 127-28.

[19]Harmon, I, 1185.

[20]*Works,* XII, 109.

[21]*Works,* VIII, 378.

[22]Ibid., p. 412.

[23]Introduction, *The Works of John Wesley,* XI, ed. Gerald R. Cragg (London: Oxford Univ. Press, 1975), p. 11 (hereafter cited as *Works* [Oxford ed.]).

[24]Lycurgus M. Starkey, Jr., *The Work of the Holy Spirit in Wesleyan Theology* (New York: Abingdon, 1962), p. 116.

[25]Harmon, II, 1444.

[26]"Thoughts Upon Methodism," *Works,* XIII, 225-26.

[27]"A Plain Account of the People Called Methodists," *Works,* VIII, 265.

[28]Frederick C. Gill, *In the Steps of John Wesley* (London: Lutterworth Press, 1962), p. 43.

[29]"Doctrines and Divisions of the Methodists," *The Gentleman's Magazine,* 9 (June 1741), 320.

[30]Maldwyn Edwards, *John Wesley and the Eighteenth Century: A Study of His Social and Political Influence,* rev. ed. (London: Epworth, 1955), p. 148.

[31]Ibid., p. 49; see also pp. 50-53.

[32]Ibid., p. 50.

[33]George Croft Cell, *The Rediscovery of John Wesley* (New York: Henry Holt and Co., 1935), p. 38.

[34]*Works,* V, 47.

[35]Quoted in Cell, pp. 67-70.

Chapter 5

[1]E. Douglas Bebb, *Wesley: A Man with a Concern* (London: Epworth, 1950), p. 123.

[2]Ibid., pp. 121-22.

[3]Ibid., p. 127; John S. Simon, *John Wesley and the Methodist Societies* (London: Epworth, 1923), p. 312.

[4]*Works,* VIII, 253.

[5]*Works*, VII, 209.

[6]*Works*, VIII, 253-54.

[7]Abel Stevens, *The History of the Religious Movement of the Eighteenth Century, Called Methodism, Considered in its Different Denominational Forms, and its Relations to British and American Protestantism*, 3 vols. (New York: Carlton and Porter, 1858-61), II, 454.

[8]*Journal*, V, 84.

[9]Henry Fish, *Manual for Class-leaders* (London), pp. 20-21. Quoted in Charles C. Keys, *The Class-Leader's Manual . . .* (New York: Lane and Scott, 1851), pp. 43-44.

[10]J. Glenn Gould, *Healing the Hurt of Man: A Study in John Wesley's "Cure of Souls"* (Kansas City: Beacon Hill Press, 1971), p. 65.

[11]William B. Lewis, "The Conduct and Nature of the Methodist Class Meeting," in Samuel Emerick, ed., *Spiritual Renewal for Methodism: A Discussion of the Early Methodist Class Meeting and the Values Inherent in Personal Groups Today* (Nashville: Methodist Evangelistic Materials, 1958), p. 25.

[12]Stevens, II, 454-55; Schmidt, II/1, 100. Some thirty-eight different types of tickets were used between 1742 and 1765.

[13]*Journal*, III, 71, 380; Bebb, pp. 128-30.

[14]Bebb, p. 128-29.

[15]*Journal*, III, 284-85.

[16]Stevens, II, 454.

[17]Ibid., p. 461.

[18]Schmidt, II/1, 267.

[19]Ibid., pp. 20, 98.

[20]"Rules of the Band-Societies," *Works*, VIII, 272.

[21]Ibid., p. 273.

[22]Minutes of 1758 Conference, in *Minutes of Conference for 1749, 1755, 1758. Reprinted from John Wesley's Ms. Copy*, Supplement to Proceedings of the Wesley Historical Society, IV (1904), 72.

[23]Frederick M. Parkinson, "Methodist Class Tickets," *Proceedings of the Wesley Historical Society*, I, No. 5 (1898), 129-35; Joseph G. Wright, "Class and Band Tickets," *Proceedings of the Wesley Historical Society*, V, No. 2 (1905), 33-44.

[24]"The Band tickets were supplied in the proportion of two to ten Society tickets." "Note by Mr. George Stampe," *Proceedings of the Wesley Historical Society*, I, No. 5 (1898), 136-37. This presumably also means that Wesley was willing to vouch for the genuine conversion of only about twenty per cent of his Methodists.

[25]*John Bennet's Copy of the Minutes of the Conferences . . .*, p. 14.

[26]Ibid.

[27]That Wesley saw community of goods as an ideal is also suggested by his sermon "The Mystery of Iniquity." Noting that the early believers in Acts "had all things in common," Wesley comments: " 'How came they to act thus, to have all things in common, seeing we do not read of any positive command to do this?' I answer, There needed no outward command: the command was written on their hearts. It naturally and necessarily resulted from the degree of love which they enjoyed. . . . And wheresoever the same cause shall prevail, the same effect will naturally follow" (*Works*, VI, 240). See also the sermon "The General

Spread of the Gospel," para. 20.

[28]"Note by Mr. George Stampe," p. 137.

[29]On the decline of the class meeting, see especially Samuel Emerick, ed., *Spiritual Renewal for Methodism,* especially the chapters by Mary Alice Tenney, Robert Chiles and J. A. Leatherman; Henry D. Rack, "The Decline of the Class-Meeting and the Problem of Church Membership in Nineteenth-Century Wesleyanism," *Proceedings of the Wesley Historical Society,* XXXIX, Part 1 (February 1973); Luke L. Keefer, Jr., "The Class Meeting's Role of Discipline in Methodism" (unpublished manuscript, 1974). Among the many books on the class meeting are: John Atkinson, *The Class Leader* (New York: Nelson and Philipps, 1875); S. W. Christophers, *Class-Meetings in Relation to the Design and Success of Methodism* (London: Wesleyan Conference Office, 1873); P. O. Fitzgerald, *The Class Meeting* (Nashville: Southern Methodist Publishing House, 1880); Charles L. Goodell, *The Drillmaster of Methodism: Principles and Methods for Class Leader and Pastor* (New York: Eaton and Mains, 1902); Wilson T. Hogue, *The Class-Meeting as a Means of Grace* (Chicago: S. K. J. Chesbro, 1907); E. S. Janes, *Address to Class Leaders* (New York: Carlton and Lanahan, 1868); Charles C. Keys, *The Class-Leader's Manual*; John Miley, *Treatise on Class Meetings* (Cincinnati: Methodist Book Concern, 1851); Leonidas Rosser, *Class Meetings* (Richmond, 1855); W. H. Thompson et al., *Prize Essays on the Class Meeting: Its Value to the Church, and Suggestions for Increasing its Efficiency and Effectiveness* (London: T. Woolmer, 1889); Gloster S. Udy, *Key to Change* (Sydney, Australia, 1962).

The reasons for the decline of the class and band system are complex, of course, and one cannot with certainty distinguish between cause and effect. These, however, are some of the factors to be considered: The rise of the stationed pastor, who gradually took over the pastoral function of class leaders; the growing sophistication and prosperity of Methodists as they rose into the middle class; the decline in the quest for perfection and holiness; the growth of the crisis-centered revivalism mentality (especially in America), which undercut the perception of faith as a continuing growth in holiness; and the tendency at times to allow classes to get too large without subdividing them.

[30]Stevens, II, 461.

[31]Bebb, p. 140. Wesley, however, at first only reluctantly gave women permission to preach. He was convinced by the results that here also God was at work, just as had happened in his initial recognition of the validity of lay preaching in general. See Leslie F. Church, *More About the Early Methodist People* (London: Epworth, 1949), chap. 4.

[32]Quoted in Bebb, p. 139.

[33]Sydney G. Dimond, *The Psychology of the Methodist Revival* (London: Oxford Univ. Press, 1926), p. 112.

Chapter 6

[1]Baker, *JWCE,* p. 2.

[2]Stoeffler, "Tradition and Renewal in the Ecclesiology of John Wesley," p. 301. Through Hooker Wesley was to some extent influenced by Thomism. "The

defense he [Hooker] offered for the role of redeemed reason . . . has since provided many members of the Church of England with a theological method which has combined the claims of revelation, reason, and history" (Ian Breward in J. D. Douglas, ed., *The New International Dictionary of the Christian Church,* p. 482).

3Albert C. Outler in Dow Kirkpatrick, ed., *The Doctrine of the Church* (New York: Abingdon, 1964), p. 14. Cf. John Jewel, *An Apology of the Church of England* (Ithaca, N.Y.: Cornell Univ. Press, 1963).

4Baker, *JWCE,* p. 16.

5Ibid., p. 49.

6Ibid., p. 48.

7Ibid., p. 149.

8Robert C. Monk, *John Wesley: His Puritan Heritage* (Nashville: Abingdon, 1966), p. 196.

9See Peter King, *An Inquiry into the Constitution, Discipline, Unity, and Worship, of the Primitive Church* . . . (New York: G. Lane and P. P. Sanford, 1841).

10Baker, *JWCE,* p. 145; Colin W. Williams, *John Wesley's Theology Today* (New York: Abingdon, 1960), pp. 220-21.

11Baker, *JWCE,* p. 145.

12*Arminian Magazine,* 1779, pp. 598-601, quoted in Baker, *JWCE,* p. 146.

13Baker, *JWCE,* p. 151.

14Ibid., p. 137.

15Sermon, "The Ministerial Office," *Works,* VII, 279.

16*Minutes of the Methodist Conferences, 1744 to 1798,* pp. 35-36, quoted in Monk, p. 195.

17*Letters,* VII, 28.

18*Explanatory Notes upon the New Testament* (London: Epworth, 1958), pp. 680 (Gal. 1:13), 430 (Acts 9:31), 850 (Heb. 12:23).

19Ibid., p. 411.

20*Works,* VI, 371.

21Ibid.

22Ibid., p. 372.

23*Works,* X, 79.

24"An Earnest Appeal to Men of Reason and Religion," *Works* (Oxford ed.), XI, 77. Wesley is saying, in other words, that the visibility of the church consists essentially in its coming together as the Christian community. The visible church is the church assembled; the invisible church is the church scattered and dispersed.

25Ibid. Wesley makes the same point in "Of the Church," *Works,* VI, 374-75. (The Latin *coetus* is basically equivalent to the more common term *congregatio.)*

26See Snyder, *The Community of the King,* pp. 35-36.

27*Works,* VI, 375.

28*Works,* V, 499.

29*Works* (Oxford ed.), XI, 518.

30Outler in Kirkpatrick, *The Doctrine of the Church,* p. 19.

31*Journal,* IV, 436.

32*Works,* VI, 378.

[33]*Journal,* IV, 436.

[34]Ibid.

[35]Ibid.; Stoeffler, "Tradition and Renewal in the Ecclesiology of John Wesley," p. 311.

Chapter 7

[1]Baker, *JWCE,* pp. 49-50.

[2]Stoeffler, "Tradition and Renewal in the Ecclesiology of John Wesley," p. 305.

[3]Durnbaugh, p. 219. I have so far been unable to find corroborating evidence for this link with Arnold. Wesley mentions Arnold's *Historia et descriptio theologiae mysticae . . .* in his diary for July 1733 (Heitzenrater, p. 495).

[4]Durnbaugh, pp. 11, 122; Littell, pp. 152, 212.

[5]Littell, p. 152.

[6]*Works,* VI, 246-47. Wesley apparently felt strongly about this. He makes the same point with equal emphasis in several places; for example, his sermon "The More Excellent Way" (*Works,* VII, 26-27), the sermon "Of Former Times" (ibid., p. 164), and the sermon "The Ministerial Office" (ibid., p. 276).

[7]*Works,* VI, 245.

[8]*Works,* XI, 479.

[9]*Works* (Oxford ed.), XI, 213-50.

[10]Baker, *JWCE,* p. 152.

[11]*Journal,* IV, 438.

[12]*Works,* VII, 158, 162, 163.

[13]Ibid., p. 164.

[14]Ibid., p. 166.

[15]Ibid.

[16]Letter to John Smith, July 10, 1747; *Letters,* II, 98.

[17]Sermon, "On Working Out Our Own Salvation," *Works,* VI, 485.

[18]Sermon, "The Great Assize," *Works,* V, 185. "Sinless perfection" usually implies a state in which it is no longer possible for the believer to sin. Wesley did not teach this. He qualified his perfectionist teachings against the charge of sinlessness in at least two ways: (1) since for him "Christian perfection" was a perfected love relationship with God and persons, based in part on the human will, the believer could voluntarily turn back and cease to live in such perfect love; and (2) Wesley defined sin, when speaking of perfection, as the voluntary transgression of the known will of God; so for him the many imperfections and mistakes flowing from human finiteness, incomplete knowledge and so forth were not sin. Wesley elaborated these points at some length. Thus one can call Wesley's view "sinless perfection" only in the face of Wesley's own specific disavowals and rather careful qualifications.

[19]Sermon, "The Way to the Kingdom," *Works,* V, 78.

[20]Sermon, "The Reformation of Manners," *Works,* VI, 141.

[21]Wood, *The Burning Heart,* p. 272.

[22]Ibid., p. 275.

[23]Sermon, "The Marks of the New Birth," *Works,* V, 219-20.

[24]Wesley, *Explanatory Notes upon the New Testament,* pp. 58, 216 (notes on

Mt. 11:5; Lk. 4:18).

[25]Sermon, "The Reformation of Manners," *Works*, VI, 145.

[26]Wood, *The Burning Heart*, p. 275.

[27]Wesley, Preface to *Hymns and Sacred Poems (1739), Works*, XIV, 321.

[28]Discourse IX "Upon Our Lord's Sermon on the Mount," *Works*, V, 387.

[29]This is a favorite Wesley phrase.

[30]Sermon, "The Great Assize," *Works*, V, 178.

Chapter 8

[1]*Letters*, II, 96.

[2]*Letters*, I, 286 (Letter to James Hervey, March 20, 1739).

[3]*Works*, VII, 275-76.

[4]Ibid., p. 276.

[5]Ibid., p. 277.

[6]John Wesley, "Ought We to Separate from the Church of England?" (Printed as appendix in Baker, *JWCE*, pp. 326-40), p. 332, written in 1755.

[7]Ibid., p. 333.

[8]Ibid.

[9]Comment on Acts 20:28, *Explanatory Notes upon the New Testament*, pp. 478-79. Baker notes that Wesley originally had written, "For no man or number of men upon earth can constitute an 'Overseer', Bishop, or any other Christian Minister, *unless as a bare instrument in God's hands.*" This is how the proof copy of the first edition of the *Explanatory Notes* reads. But Wesley deleted the qualifying phrase (beginning with "unless") from the proof copy (Baker, *JWCE*, p. 155). Compare Wesley's comment on Acts 13:2-3, where he interprets the laying of hands on Paul and Barnabas not as ordination but as public induction into service which God had previously appointed.

[10]Sermon, "Scriptural Christianity," *Works*, V, 38; Sermon, "The More Excellent Way," *Works*, VII, 27; *Explanatory Notes upon the New Testament*, p. 713 (on Eph. 4:8-11). In the *Explanatory Notes* Wesley usually employs the ordinary-extraordinary distinction, in contrast to Bengel, his source. Note, for instance, Wesley's comments on 1 Peter 4:10. Wesley often departs from Bengel in his comments on gifts. Similarly, in commenting on Exodus 35:30 and 36:2, Wesley makes the ordinary-extraordinary distinction and relates gifts to ministry. *Explanatory Notes upon the Old Testament* (Bristol: William Pine, 1765; rpt. Salem, Ohio: Schmul Publishers, 1975), I, 328-29. The ordinary-extraordinary distinction which Wesley makes with regard to gifts (as well as to offices) did not originate with him, but he took it over and strongly stressed it. See his "Farther Appeal to Men of Reason and Religion," I, Section V, in *Works* (Oxford ed.), XI, 138-76.

[11]It has been suggested that Wesley's use of the term *extraordinary* is to be understood in contradistinction to the eighteenth-century ecclesiastical meaning of *ordinary,* so that it would mean, in effect, "outside the normal ordained ministry" in a more or less technical sense. Even in Wesley's day, however, *extraordinary* had the common sense meaning of simply "outside of what is ordinary or usual" (*Oxford English Dictionary*, III, 468, 472), and it appears that

Wesley was using the term in the general and popular sense, not as a technical ecclesiastical designation.

[12]*Works,* VII, 27.

[13]*Works,* V, 38. In this connection, note the Minutes of Wesley's 1746 Conference:

Q. 2. What is the scriptural notion of an Apostle?

A. One who is sent of God to convert heathens.

Q. 3. How many apostles were there in the first church?

A. A great number beside those Twelve who were eminently so called....

Q. 4. What is the New Testament notion of a Prophet?

A. A builder up of the faithful.

Q. 5. In what view are we and our helpers to be considered?

A. Perhaps as extraordinary messengers, designed of God to provoke the others to jealousy.

[14]*Works,* VII, 26-27.

[15]*Works,* V, 38. In the latter days the glory of the church will consist "in plentiful effusions of the gifts, and graces, of the Holy Spirit" *(Explanatory Notes upon the Old Testament,* III, 1979—Note on Is. 11:10).

[16]*Explanatory Notes upon the New Testament,* p. 625 (1 Cor. 12:31).

[17]Ibid., pp. 713, 628 (Eph. 4:12; 1 Cor. 14:5).

[18]Ibid., p. 631 (a comment not found in Bengel).

[19]Letter to the Reverend Dr. Conyers Middleton, *Works,* X, 56.

[20]*Explanatory Notes on the New Testament,* pp. 629, 631 (1 Cor. 14:15, 28).

[21]Not that Wesley was totally unaware of tongues as ecstatic utterance. In his reply to Dr. Middleton he refers to the outbreak of tongues and other gifts among a persecuted band of rural Huguenots in southern France (the "little prophets of Cevennes"), beginning in 1688 *(Works,* X, 56). But little can be made of this, since Wesley gives no indication as to what his own attitude was regarding this instance. Further, some scholars have contested the common claim that tongues speaking in this case was ecstatic utterance. Several authors claim however that this instance was the first recorded outbreak of glossolalia in modern times, after a "silent period" of one thousand years. See, among others, George Barton Cutten, *Speaking with Tongues Historically and Psychologically Considered* (New Haven: Yale Univ. Press, 1927), pp. 48-66; Morton Kelsey, *Tongue Speaking: An Experiment in Spiritual Experience* (London: Hodder and Stoughton, 1964), pp. 52-55. Both authors refer to Wesley in this connection.

[22]Albert C. Outler, "John Wesley as Theologian—Then and Now," *Methodist History,* XII, No. 4 (July 1974), 79.

[23]Minutes of the 1746 Conference.

[24]See below, pp. 154-57.

[25]Baker, *JWCE,* p. 153.

[26]Minutes of the Conference of 1747, from *John Bennet's Copy of the Minutes . . . ,* p. 48.

[27]*Journal,* III, 230.

[28]Ibid.

[29]Baker, *JWCE,* p. 152.

30Ibid.

31*Works,* VII, 277.

32Letter of August 19, 1785. *Letters,* VII, 284.

33Letter of June 8, 1780. *Letters,* VI, 21.

34Letter of Sept. 10, 1784. *Letters,* VII, 238. Most Anglican bishops had fled North America at the outbreak of the Revolution.

35Stoeffler, "Tradition and Renewal in the Ecclesiology of John Wesley," p. 310.

36Ibid., p. 312.

37Sermon, "The Means of Grace," *Works,* V, 187. By "preventing" Wesley means "prevenient" grace; that general grace of God, based on the atonement, which "pre-vents" or "comes before" justifying grace. Medieval theologians had spoken of *gratia praeveniens* and *gratia subsequens.*

38"An Earnest Appeal to Men of Reason and Religion," *Works* (Oxford ed.), XI, 78.

39"The Means of Grace," *Works,* V, 188.

40Ibid., p. 190.

41Ibid., p. 196.

42Ibid., p. 201.

43Baker, *JWCE,* pp. 157-58.

44"Ought We to Separate . . ." in Baker, *JWCE,* p. 333.

45"A Treatise on Baptism," *Works,* X, 192.

46*Journal,* I, 465.

47Irwin Reist, "John Wesley's View of the Sacraments: A Study in the Historical Development of a Doctrine," *Wesleyan Theological Journal,* VI, No. 1 (Spring 1971), 48. Baker notes: "Baptism in infancy Wesley supported because it was instituted by Jesus and because it was the successor of the Old Testament rite of infant circumcision. He continued to believe that in some way objective grace was conferred upon the child of God, so that in a sense it was regenerated, or at least the process of regeneration was begun. At the same time he insisted that another form of regeneration was possible in adult experience quite apart from any sacramental rite. These two aspects of regeneration he never quite reconciled, but continued to insist on both. The classical summary of Wesley's teaching on baptismal regeneration remains his *Treatise on Baptism,* and on nonbaptismal regeneration his sermon on 'the New Birth,' first published in 1760, though probably preached much earlier" (*JWCE,* p. 156).

48John Chongnahm Cho, "John Wesley's View on Baptism," *Wesleyan Theological Journal,* VII, No. 1 (Spring 1972), 62, 65.

49*Journal,* II, 135.

Chapter 9

1See, for example, Dave Jackson, *Coming Together: All Those New Communities and What They're Up To* (Minneapolis: Bethany Fellowship, 1978).

2As illustrated, for example, in Webber, *Common Roots,* and Webber and Bloesch, *The Orthodox Evangelicals.*

3See Durnbaugh, pp. 40-51; J. W. Laycock, "Resemblance between Waldensian and Methodist Churches," *Proceedings of the Wesley Historical Society,* I, No. 4

(1898), pp. 109-11.

[4]Richard Green compares Wesley to Loyola as (in effect) the founder of a relig-ious "order." "Loyola and Wesley have points in common as truly as Luther and Wesley" (*John Wesley*, p. 150).

[5]Knox, *Enthusiasm*, p. 426. There are also striking parallels between Wesley and Israel ben Eliezer, born about 1700, the founder of the Jewish Hasidic Move-ment. See Thomas C. Oden, *The Intensive Group Experience: The New Pietism* (Philadelphia: Westminster, 1972), p. 81.

[6]On a historical and to some degree theological level, Vinson Synan has dealt with the connection between Wesley and modern Pentecostalism in his *The Holiness-Pentecostal Movement in the United States* (Grand Rapids: Eerdmans, 1971). See also Donald W. Dayton, "From Christian Perfection to the 'Baptism of the Holy Ghost' " and Melvin E. Dieter, "Wesleyan-Holiness Aspects of Pente-costal Origins," both in Vinson Synan, *Aspects of Pentecostal-Charismatic Origins* (Plainfield, N.J.: Logos International, 1975), pp. 39-80; Howard A. Sny-der, "Dialog with Charismatic Christianity," *The Wesleyan Theological Journal*, XV, No. 2 (Fall 1980). On the problem of justifying the charismatic renewal within the Catholic tradition, see Stephen Clark, *Unordained Elders and Re-newal Communities* (New York: Paulist Press, 1976).

[7]Durnbaugh, pp. 3-33; Franklin H. Littell, "The Concept of the Believers' Church," and William R. Estep, Jr., "A Believing People: Historical Back-ground," both in Garrett, *The Concept of the Believers' Church*, pp. 15-32, 35-58; John Howard Yoder, "The Recovery of the Anabaptist Vision," and Harold S. Bender, "The Anabaptist Theology of Discipleship," both in *Concern* No. 18; Franklin H. Littell, *The Free Church* (Boston: Starr King Press, 1957), pp. xi-xiii; Ross T. Bender, *The People of God: A Mennonite Interpretation of the Free Church Tradition* (Scottdale, Pa.: Herald Press, 1971). More recently, note C. Norman Kraus, "Anabaptism and Evangelicalism," in Kraus, ed., *Evan-gelicalism and Anabaptism*, pp. 172-75.

[8]Quoted in Durnbaugh, p. 33.

[9]Ibid.

[10]Harold S. Bender, p. 39.

[11]Littell, *The Free Church*, p. xii.

[12]Franklin H. Littell, "The Discipline of Discipleship in the Free Church Tradition," *Mennonite Quarterly Review*, 35 (April 1961), 113.

[13]"Upon Our Lord's Sermon on the Mount," Discourse IV, *Works*, V, 296.

[14]Littell, "The Discipline of Discipleship," p. 112.

[15]Ibid., pp. 114, 117.

[16]C. Norman Kraus distinguishes Wesley's and Menno's concepts of Christian perfection in "Evangelicalism: The Great Coalition," in *Evangelicalism and Anabaptism*, pp. 46-49.

[17]Colin Williams, p. 151 (emphasis added).

[18]"Upon Our Lord's Sermon on the Mount," Discourse IV, *Works*, V, 304.

[19]Ibid., p. 307.

[20]*Journal*, II, 265.

[21]Ibid., p. 362.

22Cell, especially chap. 3.

23John Wesley, "A Plain Account of Christian Perfection," *Works,* XI, 367.

24*Letters,* I, 286.

25"A Farther Appeal to Men of Reason and Religion," *Works* (Oxford ed.), XI, 108.

26Colin Williams, pp. 152-53.

Chapter 10

1Richard F. Lovelace, *Dynamics of Spiritual Life: An Evangelical Theology of Renewal* (Downers Grove, Ill.: InterVarsity Press, 1979).

2Ibid., p. 427.

3Ibid., p. 166.

4"Ought We to Separate ... ?" in Baker, *JWCE,* p. 337.

5Sermon, "The Ministerial Office," *Works,* VII, 278.

6Ibid., p. 280.

7Ibid., p. 281.

8Durward Hofler, "The Methodist Doctrine of the Church," *Methodist History,* VI, No. 1 (October 1967), 28.

9George H. Williams, "A People in Community: Historical Background," in Garrett, p. 137.

10Outler, *John Wesley,* p. 307. "The Methodist notions of corporate Christian discipline were derived, at least in part, from Wesley's interest in the Roman Catholic religious orders—the Society of Jesus in particular" (ibid.).

11Quoted in Isaac Dorner, *History of Protestant Theology,* trans. George Robson and Sophia Tucker (Edinburgh: T. and T. Clark, 1871), II, 211.

12Rosemary Ruether, "The Free Church Movement in Contemporary Catholicism," in Martin E. Marty and Dean G. Peerman, eds., *New Theology No. 6* (New York: Macmillan, 1969), pp. 269-87.

13Ibid., pp. 286-87. In this connection, note Baker's description of Wesley's ecclesiology, p. 71 above.

14Ibid. Another Roman Catholic author, Michael Novak, employs essentially the same logic in noting similarities between the Franciscans and early Anabaptists. "If, for a moment, we conceive of 'the Roman Catholic Church' only as a generic name like 'the Protestant Church,' " suggests Novak, "and look upon the different modes of Catholic life as sects or denominations within the larger whole, the relationships between evangelical Anabaptist piety and Franciscan piety seem more striking." He goes on to suggest the hypothesis "that Anabaptism represents a laicizing of the Catholic monastic spirituality; it is a transferral of the focus of the 'state of perfection' from a monastic brotherhood, bound by vow and cloistered by walls, to a lay, married brotherhood bound by believers' baptism and separated from the world by the ban. Its root is not a sense of sin, trust in personal justification, and aggressive social reform (classical reformers); its root is the desire to follow God completely, to withdraw from the world, and to respond to a call to a new and higher form of Christian life (Catholic religious vocation)" (Michael Novak, "The Meaning of 'Church' in Anabaptism and Roman Catholicism: Past and Present," in D. B. Robertson, ed., *Voluntary Associations: A Study of Groups in Free Societies* [Richmond, Virginia: John Knox Press, 1966], pp. 96, 99). Novak also notes (consistent with the argument of this book) that from this perspective the Catholic monastic vow and Radical Protestant believers' baptism are functionally equivalent.

[15]Ralph D. Winter, "The Two Structures of God's Redemptive Mission," *Missiology,* II, No. 1 (January 1974), 121-39, and "Protestant Mission Societies: The American Experience," *Missiology,* VII, No. 2 (April 1979), 139-78.

[16]This is in contrast to Ruether's suggestion that renewal communities exist "autonomously and without any specific kinds of institutional ties" (Ruether, p. 286). My study so far suggests that some form of institutional tie is normally necessary to prevent (or lessen the likelihood of) schism.

[17]This aspect, as well as some of the others described here, is part of the emphasis of the "mission groups" used by the Church of the Savior in Washington, D.C. See Gordon Cosby, *Handbook for Mission Groups* (Waco, Texas: Word, 1975), and Snyder, *The Community of the King,* pp. 147-58.

Chapter 11

[1]*Journal,* V, 284.

[2]Sermon, "The Good Steward," *Works,* VI, 147.

[3]Colin Williams, p. 44.

[4]Minutes of 1745 Conference, *Works,* VIII, 285.

[5]George Croft Cell, personal letter quoted in E. D. Soper, "Grace in Methodist Tradition," in W. T. Whitley, ed., *The Doctrine of Grace* (New York: Macmillan, [1932]), p. 286.

[6]Sermon, "On God's Vineyard," *Works,* VII, 205. There is an explicit criticism of Luther here for underemphasizing sanctification (p. 204).

[7]Dimond, p. 209.

[8]See sermon, "The Duty of Reproving Our Neighbour," *Works,* VI, 296-304.

[9]"A Plain Account of the People Called Methodists," *Works,* VIII, 251-52.

[10]Thomas Oden, especially, notes the similarities of modern "encounter groups" to the Methodist class meeting and other eighteenth-century antecedents, arguing that these were "the basic prototypes" of the modern movement, existing "on a vast scale in a highly refined form as a vigorous and popular lay movement" (*The Intensive Group Experience,* pp. 56-88; especially p. 59).

[11]Lovelace, p. 167.

[12]I have argued at length, on biblical and pragmatic grounds, for some form of small group structure in *The Problem of Wineskins* (Downers Grove, Ill.: Inter-Varsity Press, 1975), especially pp. 89-99 and 139-48. I would add here the importance of covenant, discipline, mutual exhortation and provision for exclusion of those who consistently break covenant in the use of small groups.

Chapter 12

[1]See especially Semmel, *The Methodist Revolution.*

[2]Romans 14:17. This is the verse Wesley usually cites when he refers to the Kingdom of God; he does not often refer to other passages which speak of other dimensions of the Kingdom.

[3]See Wesley's sermon, "The Duty of Constant Communion," *Works,* VII, 147-57. It is peculiar that many evangelicals who call the Lord's Supper a "means of grace" in practice often make little use of this means.

INDEX

DATE DUE

NOV 18 '84			
F			
MAR 3 '85			
FEB 5 '86			
FEB 17 '86			
F Oct			
GAYLORD			PRINTED IN U.S.A.